Andrée Maureau

Recipes from Provence

mary - This is so we can all
meet in Provence for a dinner
in the (hopefully) not too distant
future!   Love, Dodgie

Edisud

Illustrations by
Marie-Françoise Delarozière

Translation from the original French by
Adam R. Tolkien

Cover : Souleiado fabric
"Les Traditionnelles" — ref. 3005/1078

ISBN : 2-85744-667-5
© C. Y. Chaudoreille, Edisud, Aix-en-Provence, 1993

To my friends, who confuse
chard and cardoons
pistou and basil
sweet peppers and hot peppers
so that their approach to Provençal cooking
may be eased.

T HIS COLLECTION *is not intended to present you with every*
Recipe from Provence. This would be infinite, for Provence
is vast, from Nice to Arles, from Sault to Marseilles through the
Luberon, not forgetting Avignon or Toulon.

Rather, it is a selection, guided by the joy and pleasure of eating
in a sunny country, where we like to live well ; be it under the
arbour of a cabanon or café, drinking a pastis or two, on a picnic,
leaning against a "restanque", in the heat, sheltered from the
Mistral, in winter, in front of the fireplace, before a game of bingo,
or else around the Christmas "Gros Souper".

Do not tell me that there is no such thing as Provençal cooking ;
those who deny its existence are mistaken.

Though true that it doesn't enjoy the reputation of its neighbours,
it neither needs nor cares for it !

It is a cuisine for gourmets, sober people, be they peasants, townfolk
or landed gentry. A good traditional stew will remain the same on
every table, no richer in one place than another.

Like all spicy cooking it is a cuisine of nuances. Spreading thyme
and bay on a dish won't make it Provençal ! The Provençal housewife
knows how to develop the flavours and scents of a dish to their
maximum capacities. Only then, if need be, will she add a few
herbs to enhance the dish.

It is a colourful cuisine, full of light, with dishes that are a delight to the eyes, an invitation to sunshine.

Though most of the proposed recipes are in the purest Provençal tradition, gleaned from yellowing family notebooks, or transmitted from older to younger neighbour, others are more contemporary. And products from its soil, better here than anywhere else, find a good place on the Meridional table ; hot goat cheese with green salad, for example.

I shall speak little of the microwave and freezer. Though not at all against them, I think all the same that each cook should experiment with his or her own dishes.

Before we start, I would like to discuss, and God knows I'm talkative, the herbs and utensils in our kitchen, and our habits.

A.M.
Grange Basse

Table of Contents

At the head of each chapter, a list of the corresponding recipes is proposed.
A few blank pages will allow you to add your own recipes.
The index at the end of the book will help you make your choice.

A few remarks on olive oil, garlic and aromatic plants

Olive oil. *Judged as too strong and disagreeable by some uninitiated palates ; I suggest possessing two bottles of olive oil. The one almost pale green and fruity for salads and uncooked dishes ; the other a lighter variety for cooking. In any case, one uses very little at a time.*

If possible, buy it at an olive mill. Some remain at Oppède, Nyons, Maussane, Cucuron, etc. Moreover the owners are always charming and it's a pleasure to chat with them.

Garlic. *No cooking in Provence without garlic.*

Next you must learn how to dose it ! A "point" of garlic is the quantity you can place on the tip of a sharp knife.

White or violet garlic ?

White garlic is sweeter than its purple cousin. Buy it in the Autumn and keep it in a well aired area, it will keep all winter. Remove the germ as often as possible, digestion will be improved.

The garlic press is a very useful tool. You can crush it without peeling. Garlic is often crushed without having been peeled before being added to the preparation.

Garlic saves lives !... diminishes tension, favours sleep. Such a wonderful siesta is to be had after an aïoli !... It is also a stimulant and improves digestion, as with the famous "aigo boulido" soup.

Plant garlic around peach trees, it will prevent blistering of the leaves.

If your nails are in bad shape, rub them with garlic.

And... and... in the case of an epidemic of the plague, be sure to wear a necklace of garlic cloves.....

Aromatic herbs. *A word of advice : Better to use them dry than fresh (except of course for basil, mint, parsley...). The fragrance is more concentrated and less agressive.*

Same thing for orange peel in stews. Used fresh, it would dominate the other aromas, when dry, one guesses at its presence. Dried sage will lose its bitterness.

You must learn that everything is in the dosage of the herbs. In a successful dish you won't be to distinguish exactly between the various herbs you will have used. They must form an indissoluble whole.

Do not keep your herbs in plastic, but in paper, or a safely shut container. Don't mix them together.

Important : During the preparation, separate the herbs into two sets, one at the beginning and one towards the end of cooking.

Bay. *Dry, it is often reduced to powder, it will dissolve more easily. The leaves are often used in marinades, stews, pasta cooking-water (one leaf for the pot), pot-au-feu...*

To make excellent meat brochettes, trim small branches off the plant and skewer the cubes of meat on the sharpened wood. When infused it stimulates the stomach. You won't need much.

Basil. *is sold throughout the summer in earthenware pots or else in small jars. It flavours the markets, balconies and cars heading North.*

Large or small leaved, traditionally the small leaves are preferred. Basil is consecrated in the "Soupe au pistou". Pistou is the name of the sauce, not of the plant ! Fresh and delicious, it can be used in tomato, courgette or bean salad, and with fresh pasta. Basil, a slight diuretic, helps digestion.

Provençal "Bouquet garni". *A mixture of bay, thyme, marjoram and rosemary (very little rosemary).*

Fennel. *I don't mean the bulbs, but the wild plant growing along the roadsides. Pick it on the Saint Michel feast day (checking the leaves carefully, to avoid confusion with another plant that bears a close resemblance).*
Recommended with fish, either in the "court bouillon", or else burnt in the coals under the fish. Indispensable in "Chicken with Pernod". Medicinally, its grains are infused to drain the liver.

Juniper. *Use gloves to pick the berries, or else a metal dog comb. In the South — not to be confused with the berries of the cade plant — choose the violet ones, being the freshest.*
The berries are used in marinades, game dishes, sauerkraut, with guinea-fowl and in a certain "potato tian", delicious, yet so simple to make.
Considered as a fortifier, its berries are used in infusions.

Marjoram (or Oregano). *Grows on roadsides, marvelous aromatic herb for pizzas, vegetable concentrates, vinaigrettes and stuffing. A soporific, it facilitates sleep.*

Mint. *Wild mint is particularly fragrant. It grows very well and rapidly when transplanted North. Delicious in green salads, on tomatoes, in ice cream or with red fruit compotes.*

Parsley. *Go for flat rather than curly parsley, less fragrant. It is one of the plants that contains the most vitamins. Pureed it will rapidly produce a healthy glow, even if you make a face when drinking it.*

Rosemary. *Be careful, it is very powerful. Use very moderately. Goes well with lamb. Its short branches can be trimmed into long sticks that will replace skewers. Inhalations of rosemary will keep the cold virus away.*

Saffron. *The filament variety is best. It will dry when placed on a hot lid ; then it should be crushed so as to dissolve evenly through the soup.*

It must never boil. Add it at the last minute.

Thyme. *Pick it just before it flowers, at midday, in the hills of the Luberon, or else in the Alpilles, after a snowy winter. Thyme is good with grilled meat and vegetables, game or terrines. You must learn to dose it properly and not use too much.*

A powerful fortifier, it stimulates the appetite, eases digestion and helps blood circulation.

Some friendly advice

Don't throw yourself into a recipe before having read it entirely.
Prepare your ingredients, in front of you, on your work surface.
If, having prepared your flour, while melting the butter, when
it should have been crumbled, you realize that there are only three
eggs where there should be five, that you have no yeast and that there
is not quite 5 ounces of sugar when you need half a pound, and your
cake is successful... Congratulations ! Write down quickly how you
did it, in case someone asks for it again !... On the other hand, if
your cake looks like a flat disc, better to start again calmly, but with
the right proportions and the true recommendations. You'll be
more likely to succeed...

Don't forget *to have in your kitchen :*

A mortar, *marble if possible, to prepare the famous aïoli, pistou*
or any other pounded preparation. The pestle should be wood. A
wooden mortar is just as good. But beware ! After washing it, do
not dry it immediately ; it will crack. Choose it thick.
One or more "tians". *These being earthenware dishes, varnished*
on the inside, long or round, with a bell-shaped rim. Used mainly
for oven-baked gratins. Spinach, courgette tians...
A "daubière", *or stewing pot. This is a very pretty deep pottery*
dish with a hollow handle and lid. Water is poured into the lid all
through the cooking of the daube, this water cools the steam that falls
back into the stew.
If you don't own a barbecue... obtain **some heavy cast iron**
sheets. *These are very, very handy for mixed grills, fish, cutlets, etc.*
For this type of cooking a powerful hood is necessary, with ventilation
that is effective in evacuating the smells.

Spice and herb jars, *along with a small spice mill, or pepper grinder, used to reduce to a powder certain spices, a small grater for nutmeg for example.*

Wooden spoons.

*You are organizing a party in your home ! Your grandmother's eightieth birthday, your daughter's wedding, the inauguration of a workshop, the end of a training course... or anything else ! Why not prepare **a provençal buffet** ?*

and for yourself, with your friends, let it take place on a summer evening under a lime or plane tree, near a basin or on a terrace !...

Here are a few jumbled ideas. One must get started eight to ten days early, the freezer is welcome : all sorts of olives, tapenade, cucumber with tapenade, fougasse "aux gratelons", marinated peppers, sardines "à l'escabèche", fish-bread, a piglet terrine with juniper, "caillettes", ratatouille, bohémienne, cold caponata, spinach omelettes, onion omelettes, the twelve-layered omelettes (great success), cold pork with sage, cold leg of lamb, cold aubergines fried with tomatoes, a tray of goat cheese, banons from Banon, spicy ones, dry ones, creamy ones (not forgetting that there are some who will have developed an allergy to goat cheese served exclusively, lunch and dinner throughout their holiday and who, secretly, dream of a good camembert). Fruit, ice cream, oreillettes, praline nuts, nougat... The wine should come from neighboring cooperatives or domains ; light thirst quenching and... so fragrant.

Let the party begin...
Music !

Measurements

Your scales are unbalanced, your measuring cup has disappeared, you have an irresistible urge to bake a cake...
Then you should know that :

A level tablespoon of

granulated sugar weighs	15 g./1/2 oz.
flour	15 g./1/2 oz.
water	"
oil	"

A level teaspoon of

granulated sugar weighs	5 g./1/6 oz.
butter	10 g/1/3 oz.
salt	5 g./1/6 oz.

Half a pyrex glass will generally contain a little less than 4 fl. oz. Knowing that an ordinary yoghourt pot also contains 4 fl. oz. will allow you to make your calculations correctly !
A few proportions per person

dried vegetables : 2 1/2 oz.
rice, pasta : 2-3 oz.
potatoes : 1 kg. / 2,2 lbs. for four people
peeled green vegetables : 10 oz.
water : as much as is wanted
wine... as much as is reasonable.

Unknown cooks ! Don't be surprised at the absence of guests around the dishes. The recipes are usually proposed for five or six people. Our proportions can be adapted as needed.

A page for reminders

Aperitif bits and pieces

Celery hearts with fresh goat cheese / 15
Cucumber with tapenade / 16
Croutons or Roustides / 16
Fougasse "aux gratelons" / 16
Olives/Split olives / 17
Anchovy "quichet" / 18
Saussun / 18

Celery hearts with fresh goat cheese

celery, a cheese such as fresh Tomme, parmesan

Only save the sliced celery heart, though if your celery is tender enough, you may use it up to the leaves, this being more economical. Cut them into short sticks, fill them with the goat cheese, blended or not with the parmesan.

If your cheese is strong tasting, the parmesan may not be necessary. Add pepper.

Variation : *One might replace the goat cheese with a little Roquefort.*

Cucumber with tapenade

cucumber : 2 or 3, long and crunchy

tapenade : 1 jar, or 1/2 lb.

Peel the cucumbers. Let them drain in long pieces, bite-size, from which you will have removed the center, that is to say the seeds, with a small spoon.

Fill them with tapenade and serve cold.

Croutons or Roustides

anchovies : 10

garlic : 2 cloves

oregano : 1 tsp.

parsley, olive oil, salt and pepper

French bread : baguette, ficelle or "pain de campagne"

Puree the anchovies, garlic, herbs with alittle olive oil until you get a thick ointment. Spread it thoroughly on the bread : ficelle sliced up the middle, or slices.

Pass it under the oven grill for a minute. Serve hot.

Fougasse aux Gratelons

(Gratelons are the residue left after melting lard ; cracklings)

Either in puff pastry (Beaucaire, Remoulins have made it their speciality), or in bread dough.

Serve hot. Can be kept in the freezer.

Olives

All sorts of olives, of course ! Pincholines from the Gard, "split" ones, according to season, wrinkled and fragrant "Nyons", "Maussanes", "Greek", "Niçoises", fiery ones, garlicky ones, etc... go to the market, nibble, taste them !... choose them in the baskets.

To make tapenade on croutons, see the recipe in the chapter on First Courses.

Split olives

> 1 broom
> a pound of fresh olives, bought on the market at the
> beginning of October, to be prepared.

Whatever you do, don't taste them ! This is a joke usually played on foreigners !

Place them one by one on a wooden board, and break them ! That is to say, with a wooden mallet, split them with a sharp blow around the stone which must remain intact. At the end of the operation, use the large broom to sweep up all the olives that have escaped under the furniture !

Next put them in a large bucket of water, filled to the top.

Change the water every day for ten days. At the end of the ten days the bitterness should have disappeared.

Then prepare, in a large cooking pot,

> enough salted water (3 oz. of salt per litre), 5 bay leaves,
> 3 branches of fennel (the type that grows on roadsides),
> 10 peppercorns, 10 coriander seeds and an orange peel.

Bring to the boil for 15 minutes. Leave to cool down. Check the seasoning.

Pour the water over the rinsed olives in a varnished earthenware jar.

Leave them for ten days hoping they will be successful and good.

On the off chance, the off chance !... that they are still a little bitter to be eaten just like that, a stew will accept them with pleasure !

Anchovy "quichet"

anchovies : a glass of salted ones

garlic : 2 cloves

olive oil

bread

Soak the anchovies to remove the salt, pound them, without their backbone, with the garlic and a little olive oil. Spread this ointment on the sliced bread. In the oven, 5 minutes maximum.

Saussun

almonds : 7 oz.

anchovies : 3 fillets

fennel : 1 leaf

Pound or puree all the ingredients, until you have obtained a sort of ointment, adding water and olive oil.

Spread the mixture on the croutons. Bake for three minutes.

First Courses

Vegetable entrées /20
Aubergine caviar /20
Pine mushrooms /20
Courgettes with capers /21
Glazed fennel /21
Raw vegetables /22
Tapenade /23
Marinated peppers /24
Stuffed peppers /24
Vegetable flans /25
"Papeton d'aubergines" /25
Herb flan /26

Salads /27
Hot goat cheese salad /27
Wild salads /27
Broad bean salad /28
Chickpea salad /28

Terrines /29
Terraïeto /29
Piglet paté with juniper /29
Chard paté /30

Provençal Caillettes /31

Pizzas /31

Tarts /32
Mustard and tomato /32
Sardanaille /33
Onion /34

Fish entrées /34
Squid salad /34
Sardines "à l'escabèche" /35
Thoïonnade /35

Vegetable entrées

Aubergine caviar, or poor woman's aubergine

aubergines : 2 long ones per person
garlic : 1 or 2 cloves
olive oil, salt, pepper

Put the aubergines onto a low flame, cut them here and there with the point of a sharp knife or they will explode. Turn them from time to time for half an hour. Cease cooking and let them cool off, cut in two. Then with a spoon, remove the flesh, crush (or puree) it carefully, along with the crushed garlic, salt and pepper. The paste must be stiff. Pour, if you wish, the juice of a lemon over it. Spread on toasted or fresh bread.

Pine mushrooms with oil and vinegar

In autumn, go mushroom hunting and bring back "pinins".
Weigh out two pounds. clean them well, cut them into long pieces then make them release their liquid in an oiled pan.
While doing this, boil for fifteen minutes :

vinegar : 1 cup
oil : 2 cups
garlic : 2 cloves
rosemary : a few twigs
bay : three leaves

Throw in the mushrooms. Cook for ten minutes.
Eat them the same day, or keep them in sterilized glass jars, as preserves.

Courgettes with capers

courgettes : 2 or 3 very small courgettes per person

eggs : one or two

capers : a handful

lemon : one

olive oil, salt, pepper

Choose very small courgettes (about 3 inches long), blanch them for five minutes in boiling water, in their skins. Drain them and leave them to cool off, split them in two and remove the seeds from the centre with a small spoon.

Replace the centre with roughly chopped hard boiled egg sprinkled with the olive oil, the lemon juice, salt and pepper. Lightly cover with capers.

Serve chilled, in a large flat dish.

Glazed fennel

fennel bulbs : 6

eggs : 2 yolks

mustard : 1 tbsp.

milk : 3 tbsps.

tomato concentrate or coulis

lemon : 1

Cut the bulbs in two, cook them in boiling salted water for 20 minutes. drain thoroughly and leave to cool.

Prepare a mayonnaise, incorporate the milk, a little tomato concentrate, the juice of a lemon, and if you want, a little cayenne pepper.

Coat the fennel with the sauce. Serve cold.

Raw vegetables

The early spring vegetables are delicious and perfect for preparing a "gardener's basket" :

> small violet artichokes, fresh broad beans, tomatoes, celery, sweet peppers, "cébettes" ; with vinaigrette or an anchoïade.

Artichokes : *Take off the larger outer leaves. Sprinkle with lemon and serve with olive oil or just salt. With bigger ones, cut them in four, remove the thistle, add lemon.*

Broad beans : *choose them very young, pod them, eat them raw with a little salt.*

Cébettes : *little onions presented in bundles. eat them raw with salt.*

Celery : *serve them as sticks and eat them with salt, or dipped in anchoïade.*

Tomatoes : *raw, in quarters, or in a salad with pistou or mint.*

Melons : *cut them in two, or else into slices. Serve them with fresh figs or raw, thinly sliced ham. They could also be served with a small glass of Rasteau (a Côtes du Rhône aperitif wine), very good with melon, but also very good as an aperitif without the melon...*

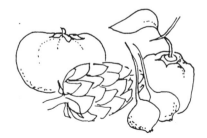

Tapenade

Accompanies aperitifs and first courses.

This preparation owes its name to the word "tapeno", meaning "capers".

> black olives : 1 lb.
>
> capers : 10 oz.
>
> anchovies : 20
>
> garlic : 1 or 2 cloves (optional)
>
> rum : 1 small glass ; or else Cognac
>
> thyme, bay, pepper, salt, olive oil, mustard.

Choosing the olives : I prefer olives from Nyons, stronger tasting but more expensive and longer to prepare. Those from Maussane are fleshier. Don't be afraid of damaging your hands when stoning the olives. On the contrary, the oil from the olives is excellent for the skin.

The capers should be thoroughly dried, the anchovies de-salted under the tap, with their backbone removed. This preparation should be made in a mortar, or else in small quantities in the blender.

Start with the chopped capers, olives and anchovies, and the finely pressed garlic. Add the herbs, a spoonful of mustard and the small glass of alcohol. Bind with the olive oil. Taste the paste, it should be either very smooth or grainy, according to taste.

To be served with an aperitif drink, on toast or little salted biscuits. It can be used in tomato salad, with pasta, or with small goat cheeses, hot or cold. One may also stuff hard-boiled eggs, after having mixed the tapenade with the egg yolks, and serve them with vinaigrette.

So, make a lot at the same time !

Marinated peppers

sweet peppers : 3 or 4, red or yellow, thick flesh
lemon : 1
garlic : 1 clove
olive oil, salt, pepper

I shall propose two ways of grilling them to remove the skins :

Either on a grill over a wood fire ; place the whole peppers on the grill, turn them until the skin cracks. Remove and wrap in newspaper for 15 minutes.

Otherwise, in an oven on low heat, under the grill for an hour. The skin will blister and crack ; remove and wrap in newspaper for 15 minutes.

Once they've cooled off, remove the very fine film of skin, the core and seeds. Then cut them into more or less thin slices. They are then placed in a terrine with the juice from half a lemon, the olive oil, salt and pepper, plus a little crushed garlic if so desired. Don't worry about making too much, for in midsummer, chilled, they are delicious.

Stuffed peppers

sweet peppers : three per person (firm flesh)
anchovies : one per person
Gruyère, black olives, olive oil

Blanch the peppers in boiling water for ten minutes. Remove the core and seeds. Fill with a fillet of anchovy in oil, a thin slice of gruyere, three or four stoned black olives, a little bit of bread (without the crust) soaked in milk, or some left over cooked rice.

Bake on an oiled dish for 30 minutes. eat hot or cold.

Vegetable flans

These recipes demand a little time but the next day, at dinnertime, it will be very agreable to have nothing to prepare.

"Papeton d'aubergines"

Tradition would have it that this was the favorite dish of the Popes ("pape") in Avignon, hence the name.

> aubergines : ten long ones, very dark
> garlic : 2 cloves
> shallots : 3
> olive oil : six or more tbsps.
> eggs : 4

Plus a tomato coulis :

> tomatoes : 3 lbs.
> garlic : 6 cloves
> olive oil, salt, pepper, onion, thyme

Peel the aubergines, slice them, let them sweat for at least an hour in a sieve with cooking salt. When dried, put them in a casserole with the olive oil, salt, garlic, shallots, thyme and bay. Place on low heat. Cover.

Once they are very soft, put them through a vegetable mill, mix with the beaten eggs. place this preparation in an oiled cake tin, a terrine or a small tian (taste it to check the seasoning). Cook in a pan of hot water in the oven for 35 minutes or more. The flan must remain creamy but not be runny.

Having prepared the coulis apart (see Sauces), just before serving, turn out the papeton, coat with the coulis, serve hot or cold.

This is a particularly elegant first course for a grand dinner, if you are afraid that your papeton will collapse, serve it in a terrine.

Herb flan

spinach : 1 lb. or chard greens, lettuce, etc...
flour : 1 1/2 oz.
milk : 2 or 3 tbsps.
eggs : 4
nutmeg, garlic : 3 cloves, thyme, bay
salt, pepper, olive oil

Cook the spinach ; I cook my spinach with the garlic, thyme and bay in the water. Dry it thoroughly. Fry in a pan with the flour. Add the milk. Stir well, adding a pinch of nutmeg and the eggs, beaten as if for an omelette. Taste and check the seasoning. Place the mixture in a cake tin. Then into the oven, in a pan of hot water for 40 minutes.

Leave it to set before removing it from the mould, serve cold, in slices or not, with a mayonnaise, a remoulade or a tomato coulis.

Variation : *I add all sorts of herbs and leaves suitable for cooking to the spinach. Radish leaves, lettuce leaves, even nettles if desired.*

Salads

In Provence, green salad is eaten at the beginning of each meal. Once the garlic has been scraped (1 or 2 cloves) on the tines of a fork onto the bottom of the salad bowl — Or, more easily, press it without peeling it in a garlic press — the salt, pepper and light but fruity olive oil is added. Toss, or "tire", the salad at the last minute.

Never forget the proverb : "carto, femo e ensalado soun jamai trop boulegado" : cards, women and salad are never shaken enough.

Recently, a new and successful salad has made its appearance : Salad served with hot goat cheese.

Hot goat cheese salad

The easiest of all : Cut the warmed goat cheeses into large pieces, place them in the salad.

Prettier : After having heated half a cheese, placed on a small slice of bread soaked in olive oil, for ten minutes in the oven, place it on the salad.

Make sure that the cheese doesn't melt too much, add salt, pepper and — why not — tapenade to the salad.

Wild salads

To learn how to recognize them is essential. In the spring, in the country, the Provençal people delight themselves with "doucette" (wild lamb's lettuce), "raiponce", dandelion leaves and wild chicory... And though the peeling may be a chore, nothing can equal a walk in the fields and a good salad afterwards !

Broad bean salad

> broad beans (larger than the salted ones) : 4 lbs. in their pods.
> shallots
> olive oil, salt, savory

Pod the beans. Cook the beans for five minutes. Leave them to cool. Remove the skin from the beans (It's easy : by pinching each bean between finger and thumb, the skin slides off. Don't crush them ! You'll get the hang of it !) and prepare the beans with the other ingredients in a small salad bowl. A touch of savory in the cooking will bring out the flavour.

Chickpea salad

Your very well-cooked chickpeas are to be kept in warm or hot water.

Serve them drained in a salad bowl in which you have prepared olive oil, small onions or scallions ("cébettes") cut into fine pieces, and salt. If you have no cébettes, shallots will do just as well.

One can find excellent tinned chickpeas. Rinse and heat them with a little water.

Variation : *it will be delicious if you add little pieces of herring in oil.*

Terrines

Terraïeto

A Provençal name for small pottery dish that used to be used for eating. Now used for small individual patés.

12 chicken livers
1 chopped onion
7 oz. of crustless bread soaked in milk
1 egg
thyme, salt, pepper, if you like juniper add 8 crushed berries

Brown the livers, after having de-veined them . Cook the onion and bread until soft. Put the livers and onion and bread mixture through a vegetable mill, or a blender. add the herbs and egg. One may add a little cream. Fill the little terrines and eat (imperatively within 36 hours) chilled.If you wish to cook them : 30 minutes in the oven, and they can be kept longer.

Piglet paté with juniper

bards of lard
pork loin : 10 oz.
pork fillet : 12 oz.
pepper : 1 tsp.
thyme : 1 tsp.
salt : 2 tsps.
juniper : 1 tbsp.
parsley : 3 tbsps.
chervil : 1 tbsp.
juniper alcohol or gin : one small liqueur glass
dry white wine : one large glass
egg : one

Chop the meat, marinate it with the alcohol and wine for a few hours. Take a terrine, bard it with lard, fill it with the mixture and end0 with a bard. Cover, and seal it with a paste made from a little flour and water that should act as a seal (this is called "luter").

Cook in a pan of hot water for at least an hour. Cool, and serve with or without a sauce, and pickles.

Chard paté

chinese cabbage : 3 bunches
spinach : 3 lbs.
pork : 8 oz. of pork loin
smoked bacon : 1 oz.
onion : 1
garlic : 2 cloves
egg : 1
basil : 1 pot
parsley, salt, pepper, olive oil

Cook the spinach and the cabbage greens in salted water, after having added the crushed garlic cloves, for 5 minutes. The white pieces of cabbage must cook for 20 minutes.

Drain, pressing well. Add the basil, onion and parsley. Chop the loin and bacon. mix everything together by hand : herbs, cabbage whites and greens, meat, pinch of nutmeg, the beaten egg.

Cook for 30 minutes in a pan of hot water in a medium oven. Check cooking with the blade of a knife. Serve hot or cold with sauce remoulade or gribiche, or mayonnaise, or else a tomato coulis.

Provençal Caillettes

They are made with pig's liver and lard mixed with spinach and wrapped in "crépine"(caul fat).

They are a little long to make.

You will have to order the pig's liver and crépine.

Here is the recipe, but try to taste each charcutier's Caillettes.

Caillettes may be eaten hot or cold.

For 10 or more Caillettes :

> spinach : 2 lbs.
> pig's liver : 1 lb.
> crépine : 1 or 2
> lard : 7 oz.
> juniper : 10 crushed berries
> white wine : 1 glass

Cook the spinach in water ; drain.

Chop up all the ingredients except for the crépine.

Make them into small balls and wrap in the crépine that has been soaked in warm water (20 minutes).

Place these balls in the oven with the white wine. Cook for half an hour or more.

Pizzas

Buy them ! They can be delicious.

Make them... following the directions on the packets of special flour, found in supermarkets.

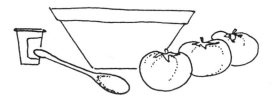

Tarts

Mustard and tomato tart

Always successful and always delicious.
For the pastry : buy it ready made or else :

    flour : 8 oz.

    butter : 5 oz.

    salt : a pinch

    water

In a terrine, mix with the tips of your fingers the butter cut into pieces and the flour until it forms thick crumbs.. Now pour a little water over the mixture until the paste becomes homogeneous.

Leave it to rest for an hour ; but if you are in a hurry you may use it at once.

For the garnish :

    mustard : 1 pot

    tomatoes : 4 or 5

    Gruyère : 10 oz.

    herbs, thyme, salt, pepper, olive oil

After having spread out the pastry in the mould, spread a thick bed of mustard, then slices of Gruyère, then the quartered tomatoes, pressed to get rid of the excess juice. One may add a few sprigs of thyme. Bake in a hot oven for 40 minutes.

Serve hot as a first course. This will make a light meal if served with a salad.

Sardanaille

A sort of large tart, the pastry is made with olive oil. Very good and very nourishing.

For the pastry :

> 13 oz. of flour
> half a glass of milk
> one glass of olive oil
> a packet of yeast

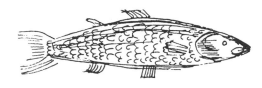

For the garnish :

> a thick tomato coulis
> tinned sardines in oil : one per person
> capers, black olives

Make your pastry. It will be rather difficult to work and spread. Take a long gratin dish. Place the ball of pastry in the middle and spread it with your fingers all around the dish. Cook it on its own for 20 minutes. Finish the cooking after pouring on the thick coulis.

Place the sardines, capers and black olives in a pretty pattern. Serve hot.

Variation : *instead of half a glass of milk and a whole glass of olive oil, you could invert the proportions : 1 glass of milk and half a glass of olive oil. Only use half a glass if your olive oil is strong tasting.*

Onion tart

olive oil pastry : flour : 8 oz.
> olive oil : 5 tbsps.
> water, salt

garnish : onions : 2 lbs.
> olive oil : 2 tbsps.
> nutmeg — grated Gruyère

milk : 6 tbsps.

egg : 1

Make the pastry, form it into a ball, leave it to rest for at least 20 minutes. Slice the onions very, very thinly and cook them until melted, at least 20 minutes. Add the salt and nutmeg, the whole egg and the milk. Cook in a hot oven for 20 minutes. Should be eaten warm. You could add black olives and anchovies.

Fish entrées

Squid salad

squid : 2 lbs.

onion : 1

black olives, tomatoes, celery, hard boiled eggs, olive oil, salt, pepper

Clean the squid, open them and cut them into slices. Cook them either in a court-bouillon for 20 minutes, or else in a frying pan, in their own juice for 15 to 20 minutes. They will be better, tastier, if cooked by the latter method. Drain them. Make a salad with them, using the tomatoes, onion, celery, hard boiled eggs, or else on their own, chilled.

Sardines "à l'escabèche"

sardines : 2 lbs.
onions : 2
garlic : 1 clove
carrots : 2
wine vinegar : 1/2 pint
thyme, salt, pepper, olive oil, bay, marjoram, flour

Clean the sardines, dry them well, flour them lightly. Fry them in peanut oil. As they are done, place them on kitchen towel, then in a terrine. Fry the carrots — sliced into rounds — in the same oil, with the onions, the unpeeled garlic, herbs and pepper. Pour on the vinegar.(Beware spattering of oil...). Leave for ten minutes in the boiling oil. As it boils, pour it over the sardines, after having removed the herbs (or not).

Leave to rest for 4 or 5 days.

Thoïonnade

tuna in oil : 8 oz.
egg : 1 yolk
capers, black olives, garlic (1 clove)

Put the tuna, with its oil, through the blender, along with the stoned olives, the egg yolk, the capers and one clove of garlic.

Place this in a terrine, serve on bread croutons, inside raw tomatoes, or with hard boiled eggs.

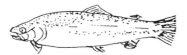

Sauces

Aïoli / 37
Anchoïade / 38
Rouille / 39
Raïto or Rayte / 39
Olive oil Béchamel / 40
Goat cheese sauce / 40
Tomato coulis / 40
Preserved coulis / 41

Aïoli

The most famous sauce in Provence.

But is it really a sauce ?

If possible, choose white garlic, more easily digested than the red variety.

Use good, but not too strong olive oil.

Take care that all the ingredients are at room temperature.

Use a marble mortar if you can, but a wooden one will do just as well ; use a wooden pestle.

Take the time to prepare the sauce.

For four people :

> garlic : 4 cloves with the germ removed
> egg yolk : 1
> olive oil : 16 fl. oz.

Pound the garlic in the mortar, with a little salt and pepper. Once the garlic has formed a paste, add the egg yolk. Continue pounding with a circular movement. When this thickens, add the oil in a thin trickle. Continue stirring incessantly, adding the oil little by little.

If your aïoli is successful, the pestle should stand straight in the middle of the mortar. Serve in the mortar.

As for me, I refuse to add lemon juice.

Aïoli accompanies cold meats, cold fish, but... it is first of all the centre of the most Provençal dish of all : "Le grand aïoli à la morue" (Codfish Aïoli, see cod).

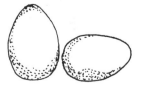

Anchoïade

This is generally a winter first course : Anchovy making one thirsty, and cauliflower being easier to get.

> 1 glass of salted anchovies
> 1 glass of ordinary vinegar
> 1/4 of olive oil, pepper
> Vegetables : celery, tomatoes, cauliflower, endives, curly lettuce
> hard-boiled eggs : 1 per person

The vegetables are peeled and raw : celery sticks, cauliflower bouquets, salad leaves, endive sticks, egg boats.

De-salt the anchovies under the tap, removing their backbone. Melt them slowly in a pot, on a low flame, stirring all the while. Add pepper, and salt if necessary.

Taste the mixture. Once cooled off, add olive oil, little by little, to taste. Beat with a fork, or in the blender.

Serve it in a sauce-bowl, a bowl, or a salad dish, vegetables all around.

The vegetables are eaten one by one, dipped in the anchoïade.

Rouille

This sauce always accompanies bouillabaisse, but can be used with other dishes using stock or broth.

> garlic : 2 or 3 cloves, peeled
> chilli peppers : 1 or 2, red, small and very hot.
> bread : without the crust, stale or not.
> milk : 1 large cup
> olive oil, salt, pepper

Crush the peeled garlic in the mortar, with the whole peppers. Add the bread soaked in milk and then squeezed. While stirring, add a little stock. Rouille should be an ointment-like paste.

Variation : *Most used recipe : without bread.*

Make it like a mayonnaise, adding an egg yolk, after having pounded the garlic and delicately adding a little stock.

For Chicken with Pastis, a fried chicken liver is crushed up, along with two or three good slices of potato, and a little stock.

If one of your guests, red, tearful, gasping, can't take the hot peppers, give him some grated coconut which will absorb the fire like a sponge. Otherwise, a little or a lot of salt on the tongue will replace the coconut...

Raïto or Raïte

A very old recipe — little used... and it's a shame !

> onions : two
> flour : 1 tbsp.
> red wine : 2 glasses
> garlic : 3 crushed cloves
> tomatoes : 6, peeled, in pieces
> capers : 3 oz.
> black olives : ten or so
> olive oil, salt, pepper

Brown the onions, cut into thin slices, in the olive oil. Throw in the flour. Make a roux with the wine. Let it cook for 5 minutes, stirring. Add a glass of boiling water, the garlic cloves, tomatoes, salt, pepper and bay. Let it reduce by half. Then add black olives and capers.

Accompanies fish, cooked first in a "court-bouillon", then for 5 minutes in the Raïto.

See the recipe for " Cod in raïto", in the Fish section.

Olive oil Béchamel

Instead of preparing your Béchamel with butter, make it with very light olive oil.

It will then advantageously accompany gratin of cauliflower, or fried aubergine, also in a gratin.

Fresh goat cheese sauce

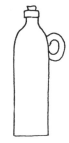

For 6 people :
>   1 cheese
>   1 yogurt
>   chervil, chives

Mix all this together. Serve chilled, with crudités.

Tomato coulis

The most indispensable sauce, when accompanying Provençal dishes.

You must always have some at hand, in jars, in small freezer bags, or tinned.

2 lbs. of ripe, round tomatoes.

2 chopped onions

3 chopped cloves of garlic

1 bunch of chopped parsley

olive oil, thyme, bay

1 sugarlump, salt, pepper

Choose a wide, thick-bottomed pan, instead of a casserole or deep cooking pot. The juice will evaporate more freely.

Heat 2 spoonfuls of olive oil, throw in the chopped garlic and parsley. Stir for a minute. Pour in a dash of water, add the chopped onions and peeled (this is important) and slightly pressed tomatoes, (they will contain less water and fewer seeds). Add salt, pepper, thyme and bay. Cook for an hour on a low flame, having added a sugarlump to reduce the acidity of the tomato.

I do not put it through a vegetable mill, or blender, I prefer the coulis to be quite thick. One can make very good coulis with the tinned tomatoes sold in shops. One should always have one or two of these tins in the kitchen.

Preserved coulis

Proportions for 20 lbs. of tomatoes :

2 lbs. of onion

8 cloves of garlic

5 bay leaves

3 packets of thyme and parsley

6 sugarlumps, salt, pepper

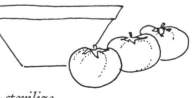

Use the preceding recipe Place in jars — sterilize.

Or put it in the freezer in small bags. I also fill ice-cube moulds and when I'm alone use one or two cubes to season pasta, rice, fried eggs...

Eggs

Boiled eggs with truffles / 43
Omelettes / 44
truffled 44 / spinach 45 / garlic ; "blette" 46
fresh tomme ; tomato 47 / harvester's ; thyme 48
"Brouillades" / 48
with truffles 48 / with tomatoes 49
Hard boiled eggs / 49
Fried eggs / 50
"Le Crespéou" / 50

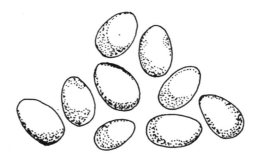

Boiled eggs with truffles

eggs : 12, for six people

truffles : 7 oz. plus the juice if they were preserved

good quality butter : 5 oz.

a little béchamel sauce

Madera : 1 fl. oz.

The day before, check the eggs for cracks and put them whole in a sealed box with the whole truffles.

The next day, peel the truffles, keep the peelings. Reduce them to a very fine puree.

Mix the béchamel (a little less than two ounces) with the Madera and the juice from the truffles. Incorporate the truffle puree with the béchamel. Cook for four to five minutes, adding a little butter and stirring briskly. Add salt and pepper.

Cook the eggs for three minutes in boiling salted water.

Presentation : Remove the top of the eggs and take out a little egg white to form a cavity. The egg white is usually not quite cooked. Fill the cavity with truffle puree. Place the rest of the puree in empty egg cups. Each diner will help himself before dipping sticks of pain de campagne, toasted or not, into the eggs.

Wine : Truffle liking Red, and egg yolk having a preference for White, choose whatever seems best.

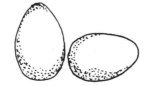

Omelettes

In Provence, omelettes are generally cooked for longer than elsewhere.

The existence of a typical dish, the "tourne-omelette" or "vire-omelette" is witness to this. It is a circular dish, varnished, without rims, with a short and thick foot, that gives one a tight handhold on the plate.

When one side of the omelette is judged sufficiently cooked, the "vire omelette" is placed right next to the frying pan and, the whole thing is rapidly overturned. The "vire-omelette" then allows the omelette to be turned onto its other side without breakage.

It is served piping hot on this dish.

One can still find these "vire-omelettes" in the markets of Aubagne and its region, and at Viguier and Tamisier in Apt.

The omelettes are often mixed with other ingredients : spinach, truffles, mussels, artichokes... rarely served on their own.

Truffled omelette

I shall start with the noblest of omelettes, but I suggest that before preparing it you read the recipe for "Brouillade aux truffes" and choose between the two.

4 or 5 hours before, or even the day before, choose your eggs : one more than the number of people, and one nice truffle.

Place the eggs whole in a sealed box with the whole truffle, well brushed if it is still covered in earth. The porous egg shell will allow the truffle scent through to flavour the eggs.

Do not make the omelette too big in one go ; for six people maximum.

When the time comes, open the box... oh, delight...

If you have enough truffles cut them in slices, otherwise grate them.

So that the truffles don't touch the pan — they would stiffen — pour in a little heated oil, the eggs, salted, peppered, beaten. Cook them, lifting them here and there with a wooden spoon, on low heat. Then, once the omelette is done — not too cooked, not too runny — distribute the truffles on the omelette, pushing them in slightly. Wait for them to heat up a little.

Fold the omelette, thus sealing in the smell of truffle. Turn off the heat. Serve piping hot.

Savour, and not a word should be said...

Spinach omelette

Easy ; 30 minutes.

milk : 3 tbsps.
spinach : 7 to 10 oz. per person
garlic : 1 clove per person
eggs : 2 per person
nutmeg, salt, pepper, olive oil

Cook the spinach for 10 minutes in boiling salted water, with the crushed garlic. Drain. Wring the spinach out carefully with your hands. Cut it into large pieces (I do this with kitchen scissors). Fry them in oil, with a pinch of nutmeg. Off the flame, mix them with the eggs, beaten with the milk. Pour into the pan. Cook on very low heat for 10 minutes. Turn over with the "vire-omelette", and cook, again for 10 minutes. It must be slightly browned.

Eat hot, sprinkled with a trickle of vinegar heated in the pan, or cold, on a picnic... It will make a change from rice salad.

Garlic omelette

Very easy ; 10 minutes.

Egg : 1 per person plus 1

garlic : 1/2 a clove per person

parsley : a good tablespoonful

olive oil, salt, pepper

Heat the oil in the pan. Pour in the beaten eggs. Cook slowly, lifting the eggs here and there, with a wooden spoon. Sprinkle over this the very finely chopped garlic, along with the parsley.

Fold it over, serve. Tradition demands that the garlic should not touch the pan, it would go bitter, and that the omelette should not be runny.

"Blette" (Chard) omelette

Easy ; about an hour.

half a pound of chard per person, whites and greens

two eggs per person

olive oil

one onion, one clove of garlic

Cook the chard greens for five minutes and the whites for twenty minutes after adding the onion and clove of garlic to the cooking water. Chop everything up roughly. Then heat in a pan to evaporate the remaining water. Also, beat the eggs together. Then mix together chard and omelette and pour into the oiled pan.

Cook the first side very slowly for at least fifteen minutes, turn it over with the vire-omelette and cook the other side, still on low heat. The omelette must not be runny.

Fresh goat cheese and mint omelette

Easy ; 10 minutes.

> three eggs per person plus one
> a bunch of mint
> a "tomme" of fresh goat cheese

Fry in butter half of the mint, chopped finely. Pour over this the eggs beaten together with the cheese (crushed with a fork). Shake the pan and scrape the rim so that everything cooks equally. Place the omelette on a dish folded in two and decorated with mint leaves.

This recipe could also be sweetened, rather than salted.

Tomato omelette

Easy ; 15 minutes.
For 4 people :

> 5 tomatoes
> 6 eggs
> olive oil, salt, pepper
> 1 tsp. of chopped parsley and garlic

Peel the tomatoes and fry them with oil, salt, pepper, garlic, parsley, let the liquid evaporate. Break the eggs and mix them thoroughly off the heat with the tomatoes. Put them back on the heat. Cook well for 5 minutes. Serve hot or cold.

Variation : *You could add black olives (two spoonfuls, chopped), capers (two spoonfuls), de-salted anchovies, 3 cloves of blanched and chopped garlic : all this chopped up together and fried in oil. This omelette will be better if runny.*

Harvester's omelette

red onions : 2 lbs.
cloves : 1 per onion
vinegar, olive oil, salt, pepper
eggs : 1 per person plus one

*The day before : nick the onions. Put one clove into this notch :
leave them in water with one or two spoonfuls of vinegar. The next
day, cut them into slices, fry them slowly and make the omelette,
mixing everything together.*

Thyme omelette

Proceed as above.

"Brouillade aux truffes "

Delicate ; 15 minutes.
Many people prefer this to the omelette.
The day before, prepare the eggs as for the omelette.

*Grate half the truffle that will be put in with the eggs. Cut the
other half into very thin slices, this is to be warmed in olive oil, for
a very short time.*

*Mix everything together : eggs and truffles in warm olive oil. Put
this preparation in a dish into a bain-marie. Check that water won't
get into the dish.*

*Heat slowly while stirring patiently, until the mixture turns
into a thick cream. Pour into a dish and savour...*

One may, to add to the creaminess, add a little thick cream.

"Brouillade aux tomates"

Delicate ; 25 minutes.

    two tomatoes per person
    half a glass of olive oil
    one or two eggs per person
    three and a half ounces of Gruyère
    thyme, garlic, stale bread

Fry the tomatoes in oil. Let the liquid thoroughly evaporate. Add the thyme, crushed garlic and little pieces of crushed stale bread. Beat the eggs as for an omelette, add salt and pepper, the grated Gruyère, and stir. Pour over the tomatoes. Stir everything together. Serve very hot, or chilled as a first course.

Gratin of hard boiled eggs

Easy ; 20 minutes.

Here is a very simple gratin, tasty, nourishing and cheap, to be served as a choice entree... or at the end of the month in a large family... as the only course, with rice.

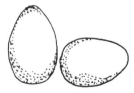

    six hard boiled eggs
    four de-salted anchovies
    a handful of capers, parsley
    a béchamel sauce

Cut the eggs in two, lengthwise.

Pound the de-salted anchovies, the drained capers, the chopped parsley. Prepare a béchamel with oil or butter. Add the egg yolks to the anchovy and caper mixture. Bind it together with a little sauce. Fill the egg whites with this preparation.

Take a gratin dish. Pour in a little béchamel. Place the eggs and cover with béchamel. (I sometimes also add capers to the sauce).

Into the oven on low heat : serve hot.

Ideas for fried eggs

You have some leftover ratatouille, bohémienne, serve with fried eggs on top.

On cooked potatoes, fried with sage, break the eggs into the pan, after having prepared little nests.

Don't forget egg Briks, but more on this in a subsequent book on Recipes from North Africa...

"Le Crespeou"

This is a succession of vegetable omelettes, placed one on top of the other and served cold.

Perfect for the centrepiece of a cold buffet, or for a light meal, served with a salad. Lots of work. Lots of admiration.

For ten people :

> 20 eggs
>
> 4 artichokes
>
> 2 aubergines
>
> 4 tomatoes
>
> 4 white onions
>
> 2 green sweet peppers
>
> 2 red sweet peppers
>
> 2 cloves of garlic
>
> Tapenade, basil, thyme
>
> parsley, salt, pepper, olive oil

Each vegetable, pureed, will be mixed with two beaten eggs.

The grilled sweet peppers should be diced or pureed in a blender. Then beaten with two whole eggs. Put the green ones in one plate to wait, the red ones in another.

The artichokes : Cut the leaves at the bottom. Cut the hearts into quarters, cook very slowly for twenty-five minutes in a pan with olive oil and thyme. Then puree, mix with two eggs and put aside.

The onions shall be fried with bay, thyme and olive oil, then beaten with two eggs and put aside.

The unpeeled aubergines should be first of all diced and fried in olive oil for twenty minutes with a clove of garlic. Then, beaten with two eggs and put aside.

Tapenade : two tbsps. beaten with two eggs and put aside.

Parsley chopped finely, mixed with the two eggs and put aside.

Now, you shall make your omelettes in an eight-inch pan, one after the other. They all must have been salted, had pepper added, and are to be cooked in olive oil.

They shall be as flat as possible, a little runny, and piled one on top of the other. Either on a dish or else in a high mould. Press down well. Alternate the colours, it will be much prettier. Serve cold the next day.

The Crespéou can be cut into slices, or into wedges like a camembert.

The mixture of all these vegetables is delicious.

You can add others, according to mood.

Serve with black and green olives.

Soups

The evening meal always starts with soup. "La soupo tapo un trau" : "soup fills a hole".

Any soup in Provence will be decorated with an arabesque of olive oil in the soup tureen, or in the plate, or in both.

There are very elaborate soups, such as the "bouillabaisse", and very simple ones such as the "aigo boulido", the boiled water that saves lives. We shall start with that.

Aigo boulido

Very easy ; 15minutes.
Each family has its version.

> water : a full pot ; 2 pints (4 or 5 people)
> garlic : 5 or 6 peeled cloves of garlic, chopped or not
> sage : a sprig
> bay, salt, pepper, thyme

Boil everything together for fifteen minutes. Serve on toasted bread in soup dishes.

Numerous variations have been added to this simple recipe.

1.

> 2 pints of salted water, with a dash of olive oil
> 5 to 8 cloves of unpeeled, crushed garlic

Boil together water and garlic. Turn off the heat. Add a branch of sage, thyme, a bay leaf, leave it to infuse for 10 minutes.

Reheat, pour into the dishes containing toasted bread, grated Gruyère and a trickle of olive oil.

2.

> 2 pts. of salted water
> 5 to 8 cloves of unpeeled, crushed garlic
> a twig of sage
> a twig of thyme
> a bay leaf
> salt, pepper, olive oil

Boil for ten minutes. Put it through a vegetable mill, into the soup tureen containing an egg yolk.

Pour this boiling hot liquid into the dishes, in which you will have placed bread toasted in the oven and rubbed with garlic, grated Gruyère and a trickle of olive oil.

3.

Instead of an egg yolk in the tureen, use some leftover aïoli. Pour the very hot liquid over this. Mix together and serve with oven-dried bread.

This last recipe is exquisite, but is not as digestive as the others. I forgot to tell you that the aigo boulido is very good for the stomach. It is always welcome the day after the night before, on New year's day for instance !

Bone soup

Easy ; 1 hour.

Keep the leg of lamb bone from lunch.
carrots : 5
leeks : 2
potato : 1
turnip : 1
celery : 1 or 2 branches
garlic : 6 cloves
salt, pepper, olive oil

Put the bone to boil in three pints of cold water. Remove the scum from the top, add salt and pepper. Cook for an hour. Add the vegetables. Count an hour from when it comes back to the boil. Put it through a sieve or vegetable mill or serve it as it is. Keep the bone to be used a second time. It will be the last but best !

Short soup

Easy ; 30minutes.
This used to be made on heavy work days, washing days for example.

> tomatoes : 5
> onions : 2
> garlic : 2 cloves
> bay, thyme, olive oil, salt, pepper

Fry the onions and tomatoes in a little oil. Once they have rendered their juices, add the crushed and peeled garlic, thyme, bay, salt and pepper.
Boil for five minutes
Add soup spaghetti or vermicelli.

Courgette soups

Easy ; 10 minutes.

1.

> courgettes : 3 lbs. peeled or not
> water : a little over 3 pints
> 3 stock cubes, salt, pepper
> 5 oz. of Gruyère or "Vache qui rit"

Boil the cut up courgettes for five minutes, throw in the stock cubes, cook for five minutes, add the grated cheese. Put this throught the blender. Season.
Serve chilled in the summer.

2.

For six people

>   courgettes : 8 little ones, nice and fresh, cut up in their
>   skins.
>   olive oil : 3 spoonfuls
>   stale bread : a handful
>   garlic : 3 cloves
>   water : 2 pints

Fry the pieces of courgette in oil until they are transparent. Add the crushed bread, the herbs, pour over this the boiling water.

Put this through the blender, or a vegetable mill.

Serve hot or chilled.

A little aïoli could be mixed in at the bottom of the tureen.

Basil & tomato soup

Easy ; 30 minutes.

For four people :

>   tomatoes : 1 lb. peeled, cut up, pressed
>   carrot : 1
>   leek : 1 small one (but don't forget it)
>   shallot : 1
>   garlic : 1/2 a clove
>   chopped basil : 2 tsps.
>   water : 2 pts.

Chop the carrot, garlic, leek and shallot. Fry them, covered in oil. Then add the tomatoes. Add water. Cook for 30 minutes, uncovered. Put this through the blender.

Just before serving, add the chopped basil and ice cubes.

Decorate with whole basil leaves, in the tureen or in the individual bowls. Serve chilled. Exceptionally subtle and delicate.

"Soupe au pistou"

I tremble a little in giving this recipe.

This soup has something sacred about it. Every housewife speaks of it with energy, discussing her recipe, the most authentic, the best !... Does it come from Genoa ? From Nice ? Should one add Parmesan ? Or Gruyère ? Dutch cheese ? Or all at the same time ? Potatoes or not potatoes ? Leeks ? Small-leaved or large-leaved basil. ?

Pistou comes from the Provençal word for pestle. Here is my recipe, without leeks, without parmesan, with small-leaved basil. It has delighted my household for a long time. Better to make a lot. If there is any left over it can be eaten cold, or kept in the freezer...

For 6 people :

a large (thick bottomed) saucepan of water (5 litres)
haricot beans, white pods : 2 lbs., podded
kidney beans, red and white speckled pod : 2 lbs., podded
french beans : 1 lb.
tomatoes : 5
potatoes : 3
average-sized courgettes : 4
carrots : 2
onion : 1
7 oz. of pasta : I take fish soup pasta : small hollow and bent

If you are unable to choose the beans, your grocer will help you with pleasure.

For the Pistou :

one pot of small-leaved basil
10 cloves of garlic
7 oz. of Gruyère
7 oz. of Dutch cheese
olive oil, salt, pepper
one may also use tomato concentrate

One morning, early...
Boil the water, with salt and pepper. Throw in the beans.
20 minutes later, add the other vegetables, after having chopped them into little pieces. Do not cut up or peel two of the courgettes, put them in the water whole. Cook for about two hours and a half. Scrape the bottom from time to time with a wooden spoon, crushing the courgettes, this will add binding to the soup.
20 minutes before three hours of total cooking time, throw in the pasta : One or two handfuls, depending on how thick you like it.
While the soup is cooking, prepare your pistou.
Crush the ten cloves of garlic (germ removed) in the mortar, along with the basil leaves, the Gruyère, the Dutch cheese (sliced thinly but not grated). Pound this patiently until you obtain a paste or ointment, that must be sprinkled from time to time with about ten spoonfuls of olive oil. Bind this with a little liquid from the soup. pour it into your hot cooking pot, turn off the stove. Serve when it is no longer boiling.
One can also put half the pistou in the tureen and leave half in the mortar, allowing each person to help themselves.

Lentil soup

Easy ; 30 minutes.
Lentils don't need to be sorted or soaked anymore.
Allow :
> 8 ounces for two pints of water and for three people.
Cook them with,
> an onion, 2 cloves, 2 cloves of crushed garlic and a bay leaf
for 25 minutes in a pressure cooker.
Put them through a vegetable mill, or blender. Serve with croutons fried in oil and a small dash of olive oil in each plate.

Chickpea soup

Once the chickpeas are cooked, fry one cut up leek and three tomatoes in a little oil. mix this preparation with the chickpeas and their water. Put it through a vegetable mill or blender.

Serve with fried croutons.

"Epeautre" soup

Long ; 3&1/2 hours.

Épeautre is a type of cereal resembling wheat. It can still be found in the "épiceries" of Haute Provence. In these times of natural products, it is coming back into fashion. I won't use the word biological, since the term has been completely diverted from its meaning. Biology is the study of living creatures, and of the laws governing this life. So what is a biological carrot or biological honey ? But let us leave this and return to our grains of épeautre.

> épeautre : a handful per person
> one bone from a leg of lamb
> a "missoun" ; a sort of large andouillette, or tripe sausage, that is mainly to be found in winter, in all the butcher shops of Haute Provence.
> garlic : three cloves
> onion : one, studded with cloves
> leek : one big one
> celery : three branches
> carrots : three
> turnip : one
> thyme, bay, salt, peppercorns

Put the bone and missoun into cold water. bring it to a low boil, removing the scum from the surface. Add the cut up vegetables and a handful of épeautre per person. Leave it to cook for three hours and a half, or else in a pressure cooker for thirty-five to forty-five minutes.

Serve as it is, with mustard for the missoun.

When the épeautre is well-cooked it will give an unctuous creaminess to the soup. Cold missoun is delicious.

Fish soup

1 hour.

> fish : 2 lbs. of small sea-shore fish, cleaned, scaled and cut into pieces.
> vermicelli or "coudes" : 7 oz.
> tomatoes : 4
> crabs : 5 or 6
> leeks : 2
> onions : 2
> garlic : 2 cloves
> fennel : one small branch
> dried orange peel : one piece
> thyme, bay

Fry the leeks, peeled tomatoes, onions, garlic and seasoning in olive oil.

Add three and a quarter pints of water. Now add the two pounds of fish and the crabs. Cook on high heat for fifteen minutes. Put this through a vegetable mill. Bring back to the boil and add the pasta.

Serve boiling hot on garlic croutons, with a little rouille but take care that it is not too strong, it would cover the taste of the fish.

Palavas fish soup

More complicated ; 1 hour.

I have added this excellent recipe although Palavas is not in Provence, but in the Languedoc. Too bad, either one is a gourmet or one is not !

fish : 1 lb. of "poissons de roche" (various small fish that live amongst the rocks, along the shores of the Mediterranean : cheap and very good)

all sorts of vegetables, as for a pot-au-feu, except for the cabbage and turnips, but with two carrots, two leeks, celery, onion, tomatoes.

Brown, in olive oil, all the vegetables chopped into pieces. Add the fish and stir. Cover with water. Leave on a low boil for three quarters of an hour. Put everything through a vegetable mill. Add vermicelli. Serve with croutons.

While on the subject of the Languedoc, don't forget to taste the "Tielles de Sète". They are a sort of little covered tart, filled with piquant squid. They are more and more easily found. Ask your fishmonger. A Tielle and a salad ; there's a meal !

Crab or Favouille Soup

An hour and a half.

a pound and a half of live small green crabs
a chopped onion
two peeled and chopped cloves of garlic
four peeled and cut up tomatoes
a bouquet garni
three spoonfuls of olive oil

Wash the crabs very carefully under a strong tap. Heat the olive oil in a deep frying pan. Throw in the live crabs. Turn them until they go red. (To avoid conscience pangs, think of your soup...)

Add onion, garlic and tomatoes. Stir, wet with salted water, add pepper and leave to cook for about an hour. Pound with a pestle, put through a tough vegetable mill, then through a sieve. Serve boiling hot on garlic croutons, with or without rouille.

Le Revesset"

(From the region of Toulon)
preparation time : 15 minutes ; cooking time : 25 minutes.
Little fish such as sardines or bogues are used in this recipe.

> 1/2 pound of chard
> 1/2 pound of spinach
> a few leaves of sorrel
> 2 pounds of fish

Place in a cooking pot the chard greens, the spinach, the sorrel and a garlic clove. Cook for ten minutes, then chop.

Add the fish, it must not cook for more than fifteen minutes. Place slices of bread in the plates. Serve separately the liquid and chopped greens, and fish.

Bouillabaisse

Originally, this was just a fisherman's soup, a family soup, containing different fish. More recently, lobsters and shellfish have been added.

A certain lay out is necessary : Fish to the one hand, the liquid to the other. Then everyone is free to mix in their own plate !

Two sauces : aïoli or rouille, according to taste ; but one shouldn't use too much, or the taste of the fish will suffer.

7 or 8 people :

> fish : 9 lbs. The more varieties you include, the tastier the dish will be : rascasse (scorpion fish), weever, gurnard, crab, sar (be careful around the prickly fins of some of these fish). Sort out the firm-fleshed fish from those with tender flesh.
> garlic : 6 unpeeled and crushed cloves
> onions : 3
> tomatoes : 4

olive oil : half a glass

thyme, bay, fennel, parsley

a piece of dried orange peel

saffron, ground or filaments (the best)

salt, pepper

Put the cloves of garlic, the peeled tomatoes, the thyme, bay, fennel, parsley and orange peel into a large cooking pot.

The firm-fleshed fish should be placed on top, cut into pieces. Pour the olive oil over this, add salt and pepper, then boiling water. Bring to a fast boil for five minutes.

Now add the tender fish. cook for five minutes. Add the saffron. remove from heat.

Serve on fried croutons, with or without rouille, mix the fish and broth together in the dish, or not.

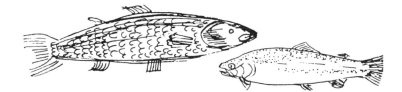

Another Bouillabaisse (with potatoes)

6 & 1/2 pounds of Mediterranean fish

a glass of olive oil

six peeled tomatoes

one potato per person

saffron, a bouquet garni, salt, pepper

Clean and trim the fish. Leave them to marinate for two hours with the saffron, olive oil and bouquet garni. Stir the marinade from time to time.

Cover them with cold water in a cooking pot. Add salt and pepper, the tomatoes and thick slices of potato, as well as the oil from the marinade. Bring to a fast boil for ten minutes. Cook until the potatoes are done. Remove from heat.

Serve up the fish in a large cork dish with the broth and croutons seperately. You may mix them together in your plate, or not.

Cod Bouillabaisse
(see Cod)

Spinach Bouillabaisse
(see Vegetables)

For your reflections and notes

Pasta

Practical, nourishing and delicious, don't forget pasta, fresh or dried, either as side or as main dish.

Cooked in a lot of salted and boiling water, into which will have been added a bay leaf and a dash of olive oil.

Pasta with pistou / 67
Macaronade / 67
Macaroni with anchovies / 67
Gratin of lasagna with aubergines / 68

Pasta with pistou

fresh pasta : 3 oz. per person maximum
garlic, basil, Gruyère, salt, pepper, olive oil

Pound the garlic and basil leaves with the olive oil.

Once the pasta is cooked, mix it with this preparation. Add Gruyère or Parmesan.

Macaronade

Accompanies Daube (stew). Consists of macaroni cooked in water and put in the oven for ten minutes with the juice from the stew.

Macaroni with anchovies.

> anchovies : 6 or 7, de-salted
>
> tomato coulis
>
> macaroni
>
> salt, pepper, olive oil

Cook the macaroni.

Also, melt the anchovies in a pot with the olive oil. Add the tomato coulis.

Mix everything together and serve with Gruyère.

Gratin of lasagna with aubergines

> aubergines : 1 lb.
>
> lasagna : according to the size of your dish
>
> tomato coulis
>
> salt, pepper, olive oil

In an oiled wide, flat, earthenware dish (the tian), place the lasagna cooked in water, and the tongues of fried aubergine. Coat with coulis.

Cook in the oven for 20 minutes.

One can add a little cream to soften the strong taste of the aubergines.

Cover with Gruyère

Serve hot.

Vegetables

I shall now start on a very rich chapter. I am actually afraid of getting lost in it. The vegetables of Provence are numerous and delicious. The sun, the diversified soil, irrigated or not, the ancestral knowledge of the growers, all contribute to making these vegetables into marvelous food, very good for the health.

I cannot recommend enough that they be eaten in season, when the market stalls overflow with tomatoes, shiny aubergines, marrows or dark green spinach.

Today, the whole year round, "progress" offers us worn out vegetables. One only has to look at them. Puffy, too swollen, forced in specialized greenhouses, they have lost all of their taste. Tired, dried out by over-long journeys, they end their lives in towns, "on special offer". Could this be, maybe and after all, the dream of a violet artichoke "country of origin : Egypt"... ?

A few years ago, other vegetables, called "organic", made their appearance. Their birth was difficult. Very expensive and full of worms, they ended their life in vague alimentary gruels, on the shelves of their owner-gardener, shaken in his convictions. Should one protect the worm or the fruit ?

Today, these vegetables have actually become attractive, along with the renewed happy face of their owner. Both have found health and taste anew, and all is well that ends well.

Garlic

White garlic, with its smaller bulbs, keeps for longer and has a less powerful flavour.

Red garlic (with violet peelings) keeps well and is strong tasting.

Hung in bunches or in braids, garlic can be kept all through the winter in a cool and well-ventilated space.

For better digestion, remove its germ. The head of garlic contains many cloves.

Baked new garlic

2 heads of garlic per person
olive oil, salt and pepper

Wash the bulbs, do not peel them, put them into an oiled dish, in a hot oven for 30 minutes. Sprinkle from time to time with salted and peppered hot water.

Serve them around, and eat them with a roast, or a leg of lamb.

Garlic puree

Cook a good twenty peeled (or not) cloves of garlic for 10 minutes in water. Change the water after 5 minutes.

Once they are soft, take the garlic out of its peel, and pound.

Add a little of the cooking water, or else some cream.

A perfect accompaniment for leg of lamb or roast pork.

Artichokes

They will, in general, be violet in the spring. They are eaten raw with vinaigrette. But there is a dish that is particularly long too make, but also delicious. This is artichokes "à la Bérigoule", from the name of a good mushroom ; the artichokes are cooked in the same way as these mushrooms that grow around Arles.

The Bérigoule also gave its name to hats worn by the people from Arles before the Revolution, they were shaped like these mushrooms, or like emptied and flattened artichoke hearts.

Artichokes "à la Bérigoule"
Artichokes "à la Provençale"
Artichoke stew

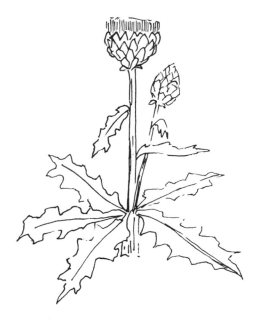

Artichokes "à la Bérigoule" (or "Barigoule")

1.

In the manner of the South Luberon. *(Lourmarin has made it its speciality).*

> small violet artichokes : 3 or 4 per person
> garlic : 1 clove for every 3 artichokes
> olive oil, parsley : lots
> no thyme, salt, pepper.

Peel the artichokes so that only the heart is left, with the leaves around it. Rub them with lemon, put them in cold water, then wait.

Prepare a stuffing with the very finely chopped garlic and parsley. Fill the hearts with a good spoonful of stuffing and place them flat in a casserole, pouring olive oil over each one. Cover the casserole, wait for 15 minutes. Then pour a glass of cold water over the artichokes and cook very slowly for an hour and a half. The water should have completely disappeared. Serve piping hot. Put a little parsley in each heart. They may be prepared the day before, since they are also very good re-heated. Serve on their own, or else with rice, or a roast.

2.

In the manner of the Alpilles

Choose larger artichokes. Cut them in two, after having trimmed them, and save the hearts along with the leaves that have been cut at less than half an inch. Rub with lemon and keep in water.

Chop up the onions (1 for every 4 artichokes). Cook them slowly in a casserole with a glass of olive oil. When they are almost cooked add 3 peeled tomatoes, the cloves of garlic (1 for every 4 artichokes), salt, pepper, 1 bay leaf. Stir well then add the artichokes with half a glass of water. Cover the casserole. Cook for an hour and a half.

The water must entirely evaporate. The onions will have become a cream in the bottom of the dish. Serve hot.

Artichokes "à la Provençale"

artichokes : 2 per person
salt pork : 5 oz.
onion : 1 big one
lemon : 1
olive oil, salt, pepper, white wine

Cut off the tips of the leaves. Split them in two. Take out the thistles and rub with lemon. Soften the chopped onions and salt pork in olive oil. Add the artichokes. Cook slowly for 45 minutes, with a very little water or white wine. Serve hot or cold.

Variation : One may all sorts of small spring vegetables, such as new carrots, potatoes, asparagus tips, tomatoes...

Artichoke stew

Long preparation time ; 60 minutes.

violet artichokes : 2 or 3 per person
onions : 2
lemons : 2
garlic, parsley, olive oil, salt, pepper
new potatoes : same weight as the artichokes

Prepare the hearts, removing the larger leaves. Cut off the other leaves half an inch from the heart, remove the choke if there is any.

Soften two sliced onions in the casserole with a glass of olive oil. Add the artichokes, sliced in half, with the juice from half a lemon. Cover with water and cook for 30 minutes.

Peel the new potatoes and dice them roughly. Add them to the artichokes along with the very finely chopped parsley and garlic (3 cloves). Check the water level. Everything must be submerged. Add salt, pepper and the rest of the lemon juice. Cook for 30 minutes.

Aubergines

I always prefer the long ones that are nice and purple. (The deeper the purple, the riper the vegetable)

There are innumerable recipes.

They can be peeled, or not.

They are usually left to sweat for an hour ; they are cut with a little cooking salt and left to give out a brownish and bitter liquid.

Fried aubergines with tomatoes

aubergines : 2 per person
tomatoes : 2 per person
garlic, onion, thyme, bay, salt, pepper
olive oil

Cut the peeled aubergines lengthwise into thick slices. Leave them to sweat, with cooking salt, in a sieve, for an hour. Put the slices, one by one, into the pan. The oil used must not be too hot. Turn them over. They will become transparent when cooked. Put them in a sieve on paper towel. You will also have cooked the peeled and seeded tomatoes, onions and herbs, letting the mixture reduce well.

Now mix together the slices of fried aubergine and tomatoes in a gratin dish. Cook for 10 minutes. Serve boiling hot, or very cold, or else on a picnic. To avoid the aubergines being too oily, a little oil is added for each slice, like with pancakes. The frying of the aubergines will take a long time.

Sauteed aubergines

Easy ; 35 minutes.

aubergines : 1 per person
parsley : 2 tbsps, chopped
garlic : 2 cloves
olive oil, salt

Dice the aubergines (nice and firm ones should be used) and let them sweat. Dry them as thoroughly as possible with a cloth.

Heat the oil in a wide-bottomed pan, and fry the aubergines until they turn golden.

Once they have cooked sprinkle with salt and a "persillade" (garlic and parsley mixture).

These could replace sauteed potatoes with a meat dish.

Aubergine fritters

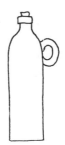

aubergines : 1 per person
fritter batter :
a quarter pound of flour
two whole eggs
one egg white
8 fluid ounces of milk

Prepare the batter an hour before.

The aubergines are cut, from end to end, into rounds, then sprinkled in salted and left to sweat.

Soak them in the batter and fry them in moderately hot oil.

If your aubergines contain too many seeds, slice them lenghthwise into very fine pieces.

Aubergine stew

1 hour 30 minutes.

aubergines : 2 per person
onion : 1
garlic : 5 cloves
tomatoes : 4
carrots : 3
celery : 1 branch
salt pork : 5 oz.
white wine, bay, thyme
salt, pepper, olive oil

In a casserole, fry the salt pork, onion, then the peeled tomatoes, aubergines sliced in their skin, salt, pepper, sliced rounds of carrot, diced celery and garlic. Add the white wine, cover and leave to simmer for an hour and a half, checking that it doesn't stick to the bottom of the pan.

"Gigot d'aubergines"

Easy ; 1 hour and 30 minutes.
Choose them large and firm.

> Aubergine : 2 per person
> garlic : 1 clove per aubergine
> olive oil, salt, pepper

Peel the aubergines. Make a small slit with the tip of a knife in each aubergine. Slip inside these the garlic, cut in two, germ removed. Put them in the oven in an oiled pan. Pour over the olive oil, add salt and pepper and leave to cook for an hour and a half on low heat.

Gratin of aubergines with Béchamel sauce

> aubergines : 2 per person
> olive oil Béchamel

Fry the sliced and sweated aubergine.

Wipe the excess oil off with paper towel. Place in a dish, cover with a peppery Béchamel. Finish with some Gruyère. Place in the oven.

Variation : My mother-in-law improved this already delicious dish by adding cooked ham, Gruyère, aubergine, etc... between each layer.

A guaranteed success !

"Papeton d'aubergines"

(see "Vegetable entrées")

Aubergines with fresh pasta

Serve fried slices of aubergine with a basil flavoured coulis, and fresh pasta.

Aubergine tian

aubergines
tomato coulis, basil
Parmesan and Gruyère

Cut the aubergines into slices without peeling them, having let them sweat. Then blanch them in salt water for 2 or 3 minutes and dry them off thoroughly. Carefully rub garlic over the inside surface of the "tian". Distribute in alternate layers the slices of aubergine and tomato coulis.

Sprinkle with grated Gruyère and Parmesan, as well as chopped basil. A small dash of olive oil, and into the oven for 30 minutes or a little more. Can be eaten hot or cold.

Oven - baked slices

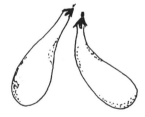

Easy ; 15 minutes

aubergines : 2 per person
thyme, bay, rosemary, garlic
olive oil, salt, pepper

Cut up the unpeeled aubergines lengthwise. Leave them to sweat for an hour with cooking salt. Wipe them off and place them flat on the dripping pan in the oven. Sprinkle with a little oil, scatter over them the herbs, rosemary, thyme, chopped garlic. Salt and pepper. Cook for 10 minutes. Serve as they are with meat. One may add grated Parmesan.

Cardoons

Cardoons, also known in the region as "Cardes", are plants resembling the artichoke. Around Christmas, you see them in fields wrapped in straw or plastic with their tuft of leaves.

They form one of the main dishes in the Christmas **"Gros Souper"**.

A fortnight before Christmas, markets and shops are abundantly stocked with them.

The best ones are the bent cardoons "prevented from coming out of the ground". They are more tender.

Everyone should choose them according to their own taste.

Cardes in white sauce

cardoons : 1 fleshy plant for 2 or 3 people

white sauce, Gruyère

Gloves : if you don't want your hands blackened.

Separate the ribs from the leaves. Remove the leaves, as you would with chard, and cut the ribs into sticks or 4 inch pieces. Put them into lemon and water as you go along.

Cook these pieces in boiling salted water, into which you will have stirred three spoonfuls of flour.

Drain them as soon as they are pliable (depending on their freshness and thickness). Put them in a gratin dish with the white sauce. Scatter Gruyère over the top. When the cheese has melted, the dish is ready to serve.

Cardes with anchovies

Once they are cooked (see previous recipe), put them in a frying pan with a chopped onion. Stir them with a little flour. Add a some more warm water and 2 or 3 anchovies reduced to a paste. Leave to simmer. To finish, bind with two egg yolks mixed with a teaspoonful of vinegar.

Cardoons with gravy

Once they are cooked, eat the cardoons seasoned with the gravy from a roast, or on their own with a trickle of lemon juice.

Carrots

Carrots with sage

carrots : a little over 4 lbs.
green or other new onions : 12
sage : a sprig
1 bouquet garni
sugar : 2 lumps
olive oil, salt, pepper

Fry the carrots — cut into small sticks — and little onions in a casserole. Add the bouquet garni, sage and sugar and moisten the mixture with a glass of water. Cover. Cook for an hour stirring and stirring often.

For a more complete dish, peas could be added.

Cabbage

As far as I know, there are no particular Provençal recipes for cabbage.

Like everywhere else, it is recommended to cook it twice, changing the water, for delicate stomachs. And for the smell, one traditionally adds a good piece of bread. If tradition were deemed insufficient, turn on the fan, and if that still isn't enough open the windows !

Cabbage and tomato

cabbage : one ; green, smooth & tender

onions : two

garlic : three cloves

sausages : one per person

tomatoes : a tin of peeled tomatoes

olive oil, salt, pepper

Cook the cabbage for ten minutes. Drain it in pieces. Then mix it well with tomatoes, onions and sausages that have been fried in olive oil.

Add salt and pepper, put the ingredients in a casserole or a gratin dish. Bake for twenty to thirty minutes.

Cabbage stuffed with chard

cabbage : 1 curly one
chard : 14 oz. of greens
flour : 2 spoonfuls
stale bread : a handful (small)
milk 8 fl. oz.
onions : 2
thyme
egg : 1
leftover cooked meat or sausage meat : 7 oz.
salt, pepper

Blanch the quartered cabbage for 10 minutes. leave to cool off.

Stuffing : Mix together the meat, chopped chard, milk and soaked bread, one egg and a little thyme. Knead this well by hand. The chard must not produce too much water. In your oiled casserole, put down a layer of leaves, then a layer of stuffing, and so on. Finish with a layer of cabbage. cover and cook for an hour or an hour and a half. If necessary, add a little water or stock.

Variation ; *"Paquetoun de chou"* :

Make small piles of stuffing and place them in each leaf. Place them on a dish. Add tomato coulis and cook in the oven.

Cucumber

Cucumber with tapenade

(see Apéritif Bits and Pieces)

Cucumber and mint

>3 cucumbers
>3 yoghourts
>2 teaspoonfuls of vinegar
>1 spoonful of chopped mint
>1 clove of garlic
>salt, pepper, olive oil

Peel and quarter the cucumbers. Remove the center, dice, sprinkle with salt and allow them to sweat.

On the side, mix a chopped clove of garlic with the vinegar. Wait for 5 to 10 minutes and then mix the yoghourt and olive oil. Mix everything together just when you are ready to serve. Serve well chilled. You can add ice cubes.

Variation : This can be put through the blender and made into a cold soup.

Courgettes

A ravishing plant, with its large leaves and flowers crying out for the sun. I wonder why they are not more often used in floral decoration.

Courgettes can be cooked in a thousand different ways, especially if your husband is an amateur-gardener and planted a few courgette-plants the year he retired. You will be deluged with them, and if you don't have the time to pick them when they're young they will become huge ; but they'll still be just as good !

They are also a gift of providence for slimming-diets. Courgettes have almost no nutritive value, so for teen-agers and healthy adults, make sure there is rice, pasta or potatoes on the side.

"Courgettes Provençales"

courgettes : 1 per person
chapelure (dried bread crumbs) : 1 cup
garlic : 3 chopped cloves
parsley, salt, pepper, olive oil

Cut the courgettes into 2 inch long pieces and slice them in two. Blanch them for 5 minutes in boiling water, drain, and place them in an oven-proof dish.

Sprinkle the garlic, parsley, chapelure, olive oil, salt and pepper over the top ; having taken care to place them skin-side up. Hot oven for 10 minutes.

The courgettes can be peeled or not. You could also stripe them. Such an easy dish !...

Courgette fritters

batter : an hour before :
flour : 7 oz.
eggs : 2 whole ones
egg whites : 2
milk : 16 fl. oz.

Prepare the batter without the egg whites. wait for an hour.

Cut the courgettes into rounds and dry them thoroughly.

When you are quite ready to make the fritters, add the stiffly-beaten egg whites very delicately with a wooden spatula.

Dip the the rounds one by one in the batter, then into the hot oil and drain onto paper towel.

Keep them warm in the oven, with the door open, until they are all ready.

Courgette compote with mint.

> courgettes : 3 lbs.
> onions : 3 big ones
> olive oil, salt, pepper
> lemons : 3
> mint in branches
> coriander : 10 dried seeds

Dice finely the unpeeled courgettes.

Put them into a thick-bottomed pot with the olive oil, lemon juice, coriander, onions, salt and pepper.

Simmer on low heat for 15 minutes. Leave the dish to cool down.

Serve chilled with the chopped (you can do this with scissors) mint leaves.

Courgette pancakes

> courgettes : 2 average ones
> garlic : 2 chopped cloves
> flour : 1 tbsp.
> cream : 1 pot
> egg : 1
> salt, pepper

Grate finely the fresh courgettes in their skins. Press them in a cloth to get rid of the excess liquid. Put them aside.

Mix together the flour, egg and cream to obtain a pancake batter. Add the courgettes and chopped garlic. Season.

Cook as you would ordinary pancakes. As you go along, keep them in the oven with its door open.

Courgette gratin with tomatoes

>courgettes : 2 lbs
>tomatoes : 1 lb
>meat : 3/4 lb. of stuffing or chopped meat
>egg : 1
>olive oil, salt, pepper

Soften the onions and courgettes in a pan. Mix in the meat and simmer.

Put the courgettes and stuffing into a tian, then cover with fresh tomatoes.

Cook for 30 minutes. Serve hot or cold.

Courgette tian (hot or cold)

>courgettes : 2 lbs.
>onions : 2 lbs.
>salt, pepper, olive oil, flour, 2 eggs, Gruyère, nutmeg.

Soften in olive oil the sliced onions in a cooking pot. Add the courgettes. Stir well.

When they're almost cooked, toss in the grated cheese, add salt and pepper.

Pour into a gratin dish after having mixed in a spoonful of flour, a pinch of nutmeg and two whole eggs.

Courgette tian with basil

Prepare the courgettes as in the above recipe, but without onion and with lots of chopped up basil leaves.

Courgette tian with sausage meat

courgettes

onions

sausage meat : 7 oz.

thyme, bay, salt, pepper, olive oil

Gruyère

Fry the pieces of courgette together with the onions. Add the roughly chopped sausage meat, thyme and bay. Fry this well in the pan. Mix well and pour into a gratin dish. Add a little water or stock if it seems too dry. Powder with Gruyère and cook for 20 minutes.

Courgette flower fritters

Batter :

flour : 4 oz.

olive oil : 2 tbsps.

water : 1 glass of warm water

baking powder

egg : 1 egg white

salt

courgette flowers : 3 per person

Make your pastry with the tips of your fingers, add the stiffly beaten white at the end of the operation. Stir. Lift delicately. Leave it to rest for an hour.

Dip in the flowers (pistil removed) one by one and fry.

Stuffed courgette flowers

very fresh flowers : 3 per person ; preferably, if you have a garden, choose male flowers. (They don't taste any better, but they don't produce any courgettes either !)

tomatoes : 6, for the coulis

courgettes : 3 small ones

egg : 1

chapelure (dried bread crumbs) : 2 tbsps.

lemons :2

garlic : 2 cloves

basil, mint, parsley

olive oil, salt, pepper

Chop the herbs and garlic and blend with the small courgettes. Fry slowly in olive oil, so that the water evaporates. Leave to cool off. Then incorporate the egg and chapelure. Make the tomato coulis.

Garnish each flower with stuffing and close the petals. Next, arrange them in a dish and cook in a hot oven for twenty minutes. Pour chicken stock over them.

Serve hot or cold, with the coulis and a few mint and basil leaves. Lots of work... Loads of success !

Spinach

One usually needs about a 3/4 pound per person. The most traditional dish is the :

Spinach tian

Particularly in the Comtat of Avignon and in Carpentras.

> spinach : 2 lbs of very young spinach
> flour : 2 tbsps
> olive oil : 3 tbsps
> 1/2 a glass of milk
> hard boiled eggs : 3
> black olives : about ten
> garlic : 2 cloves of garlic
> parsley, salt, pepper

Sort the spinach (I never bother removing the tails, just the stalks). Wash and drain well, cut into little pieces.

Put the spinach into a salad bowl, with salt, pepper, olive oil, chopped garlic and parsley and the flour. Mix everything together, adding the olives and eggs.

Pour into a tian and dust with bread crumbs. Cook for two hours in an oven on low heat.

One can add chard greens, radish leaves to the spinach.

Spinach bouillabaisse

for four people :

>   spinach : 2 lbs.
>   potatoes : 2 lbs.
>   garlic : 4 cloves
>   eggs : 4 (1 per person)
>   salt, pepper, olive oil

Soften in oil the raw spinach. Add the quartered potatoes, crushed garlic, salt and pepper.

Fry, without forgetting to stir, then add cold water to cover.

Cook for twenty minutes. Poach the eggs in stock. Eat it all together in soup plates, or if you prefer start with the eggs in stock, then the vegetables.

Codfish tian with spinach

see Cod

Sardines with spinach

see Sardines

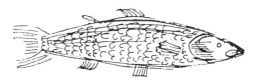

Fennel

Glazed fennel

see First Courses

Fennel and tomato

fennel : 6
onions : 1
salt pork
garlic : 5 cloves
bay : 2 leaves
tomatoes : 6
white wine
salt, pepper, olive oil

Brown the onions in quarters, with the boiled salt pork.

Add the halved fennel bulbs, garlic, white wine, pressed tomatoes, salt, pepper and bay leaves. Simmer for an hour and a half.

Serve hot or cold.

Haricot beans

Navarin of fresh haricot beans

>lamb : 1 diced shoulder of lamb and 1 lb. of neck (adds taste)
>
>fresh haricot beans : 2 lbs., crushed
>
>tomatoes : 4 or 5
>
>onions : 2
>
>garlic : 3 cloves
>
>thyme, bay, salt, pepper, olive oil

Brown the meat on all sides in olive oil with the onions for five minutes, add the tomatoes, herbs, beans.

Add salt and pepper and cook in a cast iron casserole for an hour and a half, taking care that the food doesn't stick to the bottom of the pan. Add a little water.

Serve boiling hot.

Haricot bean tian

>beans : 2 lbs. of beans that have been soaking for 24 hours
>
>pork cutlet or salt pork
>
>sage, bouquet garni, onion
>
>salt, pepper, olive oil

Brown the pork cutlets. Place them in the bottom of a casserole with olive oil and the sliced onions. Pour over the beans and stock.

Cook for 3 hours, or 40 minutes in a pressure cooker.

French beans

In springtime :

"Pois gourmands"

Choose :

2 lbs. of very fresh "haricots verts"
1 onion
7 oz. of salt pork
some flour
3 egg yolks
olive oil

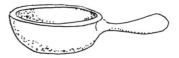

Remove the strings from the beans. Cook them very slowly for ten minutes in a covered pot, into which you will have added the olive oil, chopped salt pork and sliced onion.

Dust with flour, wet the mixture with a pint of stock. Cook until the sauce has disappeared. Serve like it is, or else add three egg yolks, bound with the juice.

French bean salad

Cook them in handfuls in boiling water (Throw in a handful, wait for the water to come back to the boil, put in another handful and so on. Uncovered). Don't cook them too long, they should remain crunchy.

In the same water, and at the same time, cook some potatoes in their skin. Then peel them and cut them into rounds. Mix them with the beans and season with olive oil and a good quantity of pressed garlic and salt. Serve warm. It will be delicious and is a complete meal with a slice of ham or cold meat.

French beans and tomatoes

    beans : 2 and 3/4 pounds
    tomatoes : 3
    onions : 2
    parsley, salt, pepper, olive oil

Fry the sliced onions, then the beans in a casserole. Pour in 1/2 a glass of water and cook covered for 20 minutes. Add the chopped tomatoes, cover and cook for 30 minutes. The liquid should be quite reduced.

Can be eaten cold with a little basil, or hot if preferred.

French beans "Coco plat"

Remove the strings and pod any beans that seem too large. Cook them in boiling water a handful at a time (The water must come back to the boil for each handful).

Don't cook for too long.

Drain them. Serve them with some butter and parsley or olive oil.

Marrow or Pumpkin

Not terribly nourishing but so pretty !

You can prepare it as a soup that will be served in the emptied-out marrow itself. You have to cut out a hat from the top of the marrow and then empty it out with a knife and spoon which is quite difficult. The soup is made with pieces of marrow, potatoes, two onions for 25 ounces of marrow and 25 ounces of potato that have been softened in a little oil for five minutes. You then cover with water, along with a bay leaf, a piece of celery, a pinch of nutmeg and salt. Cook for twenty minutes, then crush with a fork or potato-masher. Cream is then added, and the whole thing is poured back into the marrow. Take care that it doesn't leak ! The hat is used as a lid. One could make a hole in it for the ladle. This soup should be eaten nice and hot.

Marrow tian

sliced marrow : 3 lbs.
olive oil, salt, pepper, bay, nutmeg
eggs : 3
milk : 8 fl. oz.
garlic : 1 clove
grated Gruyère

Cook your pieces of marrow with the chopped garlic in a little oil. The marrow will lose its liquid. Then put it through a vegetable mill. Fry a sliced onion with a spoonful of flour and the milk.

Mix all this together, marrow and roux, adding two beaten eggs, bay, pinch of nutmeg, salt and pepper. Sprinkle with Gruyère and dried bread-crumbs. Put in the oven, on low heat, and proceed as for a gratin.

Onions

They are to be found in almost every dish. White ones for salad, yellow for cooked dishes. Don't forget "cébettes" (scallions) in spring, to be eaten raw, or else added to dishes, at the last minute, chopped into small pieces.

Onions stuffed with garlic

onions : 2 lbs.

garlic : 6 cloves

salt, pepper, olive oil

In a pressure cooker, blanch the whole onions for 4 minutes. Dig a hole in them. Mix the interior of the onions with the garlic, chopped, or not, and garnish the emptied onion with this mixture. Cook in the oven for 15 minutes, thermostat 7 - 8.

Roast onions

white onions : 1 per person

sage

bay

olive oil, salt, pepper

Blanch the onions for 5 to 10 minutes and let them cool off. Make two cuts in each of them. In the one, put a piece of bay leaf and in the other, a sprig of sage.

Put the onions in a tian. Sprinkle with oil and cook in an oven on low heat for 2 hours. Baste regularly.

An exquisite garnish for certain roasts.

Leeks

Excellent in autumn or winter.

Leek sauce with cod
(see Cod)

Leeks in vinaigrette
Everyone knows how to make this.

Sweet peppers

You will find different species. The very expensive small green ones for salads. Then the larger ones, with thicker flesh ; red, yellow, green...

Marinated peppers
See First courses

Stuffed peppers

Stuffing :

  10 oz. of sausagemeat
  1 onion
  1 good slice of bread
  1 egg yolk
  dried bread crumbs
  olive oil, salt, pepper

Heat the onions in the oven, then peel them. Fill them with the stuffing, cooked seperately. Place them in an oven-proof dish, sprinkle with the bread crumbs (chapelure) and cook for 15 minutes. Add a few tomatoes to make a little juice, or else a little water, or stock.

To stuff the peppers, you only need to cut off the top and stem. One can lay them flat or standing like pillars, striped like Buren's black and white ones in Paris.

Potatoes

The potatoes from the high valley of the Calavon are very good, and those from the region of Pertuis enjoy a very good reputation.

Baked in their skin, their "robe des champs" (their field gown), with a trickle of olive oil and some salt ! What could be better !...

Or else in a stew with black olives and garlic.

Stew

Fry together black olives and unpeeled but crushed cloves of garlic, with a bay leaf. Add the peeled and diced potatoes. Cover with water and cook for 20 minutes.

Potato tian with juniper

potatoes : 2 lbs.

juniper : 20 berries

bacon and salt pork

olive oil, salt, pepper, dried bread crumbs

Place potato rounds (peeled and not too thin) in an oiled gratin dish.

Crush or chop up the juniper berries with the salt pork. Alternate a row of potatoes with a row of mixed juniper and salt pork until the dish is filled.

Cover with plentifully peppered water. Cover the dish — or not — with a sheet of aluminium. Cook au gratin with the bread crumbs.

Provençal potato tian

    potatoes : 2 lbs
    onions : 10 oz.
    tomatoes : 1 lb.
    garlic, thyme, bay
    olive oil, salt, pepper

Place a layer of potatoes in a tian, then a little pressed garlic, thyme, a layer of tomatoes and a layer of onions. And start again...

Add a little stock if the tomatoes aren't very juicy.

Variations : One could add pieces of lamb (breast or rib) between layers.

One could leave out the tomatoes.

One could also add sweet peppers.

In any case, sprinkle with a good helping of thyme, and lots of pepper.

An extra variation : Fry the onions and tomatoes together, as if you were making a coulis, and spread this coulis between the layers of potato.

A word of advice on "frites"

You can throw crushed garlic cloves into the french-fried potatoes' second frying oil.

Tomatoes

There is no such thing as Provençal cuisine without tomatoes.

It is a difficult day for the Provençal when she heads North !

The best season for tomatoes is the Summer. Avoid the imported and tasteless winter ones. You will be better off using tinned tomatoes ; they will be peeled seeded and sometimes seasoned, either with basil or with thyme.

Tomatoes go well with almost all vegetables, peppers, onions, courgettes, aubergines.

Stuffed tomatoes

Either

with courgettes and chopped meat. The mixture will have been fried in olive oil with a chopped onion. The tomatoes will be filled with it before going into the oven.

Or,

with meat or stuffing, browned in olive oil and mixed with a little bread soaked in milk.

Or else,

with sausagemeat cooked with onion, the flesh from the tomatoes and a large spoonful of uncooked rice that will have been placed in the bottom of each emptied tomato.

Take care. In any case, dig out your round tomatoes. Salt the insides. Let them rest for half an hour, then turn them over onto some paper towel, or onto a grill to drain.

Tomatoes "à la Provençale"

The true recipe demands an hour or an hour and a half cooking time.

tomatoes : 2 or 3 per person

garlic, salt, olive oil, parsley, pepper.

If you have the time I would advise you to follow the recipe ; but if you are in a hurry, do it as you wish, more rapidly.

Cut the tomatoes in two, and seed them. Lay the tomatoes cut side down. Cover and cook for 15 minutes. Turn them over carefully, away from the heat. Cover with the very finely chopped garlic and parsley, a pinch of sugar, salt and pepper.

Then put the pan back on the heat and watch over the cooking for an hour. It must cook very slowly. Add cold water, in teaspoonfuls.

There will be just mouthfuls of tomato, shriveled up and exquisite.

You may prefer to cook them in the oven : they will be easier on the digestion ; in this case add chapelure (dried bread crumbs).

These tomatoes keep very well in the freezer.

Mixed vegetable dishes

Ratatouille

Ratatouille is one of the most famous dishes. To every household its own recipe, and to each recipe its particular taste.

It is up to you to add new ones.

The old tradition demands that one cook each vegetable separately. And truly this is the secret of the dish.

courgettes : 2 lbs.
aubergines : 3 lbs.
tomatoes : 3 lbs.
sweet peppers : 2 lbs.
onions : 1 lb.
garlic : 3 cloves
salt, pepper, thyme, bay, olive oil

Cook the peeled vegetables (tomatoes pressed and seeded) separately for 30 minutes in olive oil.

Gather the cooked vegetables together. Add the garlic, salt and pepper and cook for another 30 minutes.

Delicious, whether hot or cold.

You could break eggs into it to make a more substantial dish.

Bohémienne

Resembles ratatouille, but only tomatoes and aubergines are used in the making.

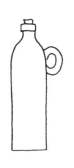

aubergines : 2 lbs.
tomatoes : 2 lbs.
onions : 2
anchovies in oil : 8
garlic : 3 cloves
olive oil : 1 glass
flour : 1 spoonful
milk : 1/2 a glass

Dice the peeled aubergines. Salt and drain for thirty minutes. Peel and seed the tomatoes. Soften the sliced onions in a casserole. Add the aubergines. Stir well. Add the tomatoes and garlic and cook slowly, stirring so that nothing sticks to the bottom of the pan, and crushing the vegetables against the sides of the casserole. It must make a sort of paste. This should take at least 45 minutes, maybe a little longer.

On the side, you will have crushed the anchovies with the flour and milk. Add this mixture to the Bohémienne. Mix it thoroughly together.

If you wish to cook this au gratin, put it in the oven, otherwise serve it hot or cold, with melted Gruyère.

Caponata or Caponate

a variation on the preceding recipes.

aubergines : 1 lb.

sweet peppers : 1 lb.

tomatoes : 1 lb.

onions : 1 lb.

wine vinegar

olives, capers, salt, pepper, olive oil.

First of all, soften the onions, then add the peeled and drained aubergines. Mix everything together. Cook without covering, add salt, pepper, olives.

Once the dish is cooked, add a spoonful of wine vinegar and some capers. Serve hot or cold.

All these dishes keep in the freezer.

I will approach Moussaka, an aubergine dish with lamb, in the Mediterranean recipes.

Fish

Cod / *108*
brandade 109 / aïoli 110 / bouillabaisse 111
cod with spinach 111 / cod with leeks 112 / cod in Raïte 112
Shad / *113*
Sea bream / *113*
with garlic 113 / roasted 114
Mussels / *115*
"marinière" 115 / fried 116 / brochettes 116 / pilau 117
Fishbread / *117*
Red Mullet / *118*
grilled 118 / "en papillotte" (cooked in tinfoil) 118
in raw ham papillottes 119
Sardines / *120*
deep-fried 120 / gratin with spinach 121
gratin with pine nuts 122 / gratin with tomatoes 122
Fish "Sartagnade" / *123*
Tuna / *123*
fresh, with tomatoes 123 / "à la bonne femme" 124
Chartreuse 124

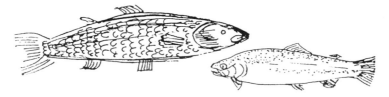

Cod

has an important place in the cooking of the Midi. Being cheap, it allowed people who were not well-off to have fish. Sold in salt fillets, it could travel without going bad. Today, it has become relatively expensive, and the fish travels very well, refrigerated...

All the same, cod still has its place in the hearts (and stomachs) of the Provençal people and, around Good Friday, any self-respecting Provençal grocery will have, up for sale, de-salted cod and soaked chickpeas for the famous aïoli, of which it is the centre.

True cod-amateurs prefer it dry, and salted. In this case, choose thick pieces.

The fillets sold in plastic, though more practical, are not as good.

In any case, it must be de-salted at least 24 hours in advance for the dried fish. 12 hours will suffice for the fillets.

The day before, you must put the cod, without having removed its skin, in a raised sieve, in a basin full of water, skin side up (you can do this by simply putting a stone or upside-down plate in the basin). The dissolved salt will descend to the bottom. Change the water two or three times during the twenty-four hours (or the twelve hours for the fillets).

Drain, put the fish into very cold water, and bring to the boil. But be careful! Cod won't stand a strong boil. You must watch over it.

The water mustn't boil, but simmer very slightly for a few minutes. Turn off the cooker and let it poach for fifteen minutes in the water.

Cod has given birth to two great and very traditional recipes :
Aïoli
Brandade

Brandade

Every household has its secrets. To start anew on the discussion over the use of garlic or not would be exhausting and vain. On the other hand, the presence of truffles is unanimously called for. As for that of potatoes, it is criticized or banished.

This is my "potato-less" recipe.

Cook the cod as above.

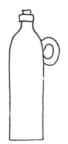

> cod : 1 lb. per person
>
> olive oil : 8 fl. oz.
>
> milk : 8 fl. oz.
>
> pepper, a tiny pinch of nutmeg
>
> truffles, or not

Once the cod has been poached, remove the bones, but not the skin. Keep the pieces on low heat, as well as the milk and nutmeg.

Pound the cod as it breaks into little pieces. The skin adds to the creaminess of the preparation.

Pour into a thick bottomed pot and stir constantly, adding warm milk and oil little by little. A thick and creamy paste will be obtained.

Add one or two truffles, cut into rounds, and pepper.

Place the brandade in a bain-marie (double-boiler) and serve with fried croutons.

This entrée could also be served in small vol-au-vents, made with flaky pastry.

The town of Nîmes, in the Languedoc, specializes in the preparation of the brandade. Excellent tins of it are to be found there.

"Le Grand Aïoli"

See the recipe for the sauce in the "Sauces" chapter.

A one-dish meal, where the vegetables cooked in water are presented round the the cod, usually poached, but sometimes fried. A festive meal !...

cod : 5 to 7 oz. per person

hard-boiled eggs : 1 per person

with a cornucopia of vegetables : cauliflower, potatoes, carrots, french beans, beetroot, chickpeas, artichokes...

snails cooked in water. Choose a good quality tin from Burgundy.

The Aïoli : see Sauces, served in a mortar.

The cod : de-salted, poached, served warm.

The vegetables : cook them in boiling water separately, so that they retain their flavour and serve them warm. This is a little last-minute problem, allow for various sieves to be placed on pots that are cooking other vegetables. Take particular care with the cauliflower : cook it strictly apart, because of its strong smell.

Bring the large dishes to the table once everyone is seated to avoid allowing the food to get cold.

Bon appetit !

Cod bouillabaisse

        cod : 7 oz. per person, cooked
        onions : 2, chopped
        tomatoes : 4 or 5
        garlic : 6 cloves
        thyme, parsley, saffron, pepper, fennel, bay
        potatoes : 1 per person
        eggs : 1 hard-boiled egg for every two people
        pieces of orange peel and slices of stale bread

Brown the onions. Add the peeled tomatoes, pressed garlic, fennel, bay, orange peel, herbs and pepper. Stir well. Then add the thick slices of potato and enough of the cod's cooking water to cover.

Cook for 25 to 30 minutes. Add the warm cod and saffron. Simmer gently, and serve on slices of bread, decorated with half a hard-boiled egg. Can be served with aïoli.

Be careful; the potatoes must not break. Watch over the simmering.

Cod with spinach

Easy; 1 hour.

        cod : 3 or 4 oz. pre person
        anchovies : 2 or 3
        spinach : 2 lbs.
        salt, pepper, dried bread crumbs, olive oil

Poach the cod and cut it into pieces. De-salt the anchovies under a trickle of tap water and reduce them to a puree that will be mixed in with the spinach. Cook the spinach, press to drain, cut into pieces. In an oiled gratin dish, place a layer of spinach, a layer of cod, and so on. Finish with a layer of spinach. Trickle a little olive oil over the dish and dust with dried bread crumbs. You could also pour over a little milk or cover with a béchamel sauce.

Cod with leeks

A very traditional Haute-Provence dish on Christmas eve. A rustic and delicious dish.

> leeks : 6 lbs.
> hard-boiled eggs : 1 per person
> cod : 3 oz. per person
> black olives : a handful
> truffles : 1 or 2
> olive oil, pepper, dried bread crumbs

Stone the olives and chop them up.

Poach the cod, crumble it up and keep it warm. Blanch the leeks for 5 minutes. Cut them into pieces and put them in a casserole with three spoonfuls of olive oil. Cover and reduce on low heat, at least 15 minutes, or until you obtain a thick cream.

Add the bowl of black olives and the flakes of cod, with a little of its cooking water. Let it simmer for 45 minutes, without boiling. Pour dried bread crumbs (a bowlful) over it ; it will swell. Then mix everything together thoroughly. Check the seasoning and add pepper, if necessary.

Cod in Raïte (or raïto)

> cod : 3 oz. per person, de-salted.
> onion : 1
> flour : 1 tbsp.
> red wine : 16 fl. oz.
> boiling water : 16 fl. oz.
> garlic : 2 pounded cloves
> parsley
> tomatoes : 3, peeled and reduced
> olive oil

Fry the onion. Add the flour, stir. Pour in the wine and boiling water. Stir as if for a roux. Bring to the boil and add the herbs, tomatoes and garlic. Leave it to reduce. The sauce should be sick.

After de-salting the cod, roll it in flour, deep-fry it. Then arrange the deep fried cod-pieces in the wine sauce, and add a good handful of capers. Leave it to simmer very gently and serve.

Shad

This is a fish that has unfortunately disappeared from the Avignon riverbanks, though still frequently found in Morocco, being unable to swim up the Rhône because of dams. Caught in "vire-vire" along the shores of the river, they heralded the spring in the kitchens of the region.

Shad with sorrel.

Sea bream

with garlic

Easy ; 1 hour

Sea bream : about 3 lbs.
garlic : 15 cloves
salt, pepper, olive oil, fennel

Scale and clean the fish. Sprinkle salt and pepper over the insides. Slip in the crushed but unpeeled cloves of garlic.

Put the fish in the oven, laid on fennel branches, with a little olive oil.

Cook for 45 minutes, basting it often, at a moderate temperature.

Roasted sea bream with potatoes

Long preparation-time.
Cooking-time : 45 minutes

> average-sized, nicely rounded sea bream
> 1 or 2 potatoes per person
> 2 or 3 onions
> 5 tomatoes
> a handful of black olives
> bay, thyme, dry fennel

You could make this into a whole meal with a large fish.

Pour the olive oil into the dish, or else straight into the dripping pan if you have a large sea bream, and arrange quite thick slices of potato, then sliced onions, thyme, bay and peeled tomatoes. Add the black olives, salt and pepper. Cook on low heat for 15 minutes. Then place on top the sea bream, scaled, cleaned, oiled and salted. Do not cut open it's back, or the flavour will escape.

Watch over the cooking (30 to 60 minutes, depending on the size of the fish). Baste the fish often.

Serve.

Mussels

I love those from Bouzigues.

Mussels "à la marinière"

mussels : about a pound a person
shallots : 2
parsley
white wine : 1 glass
flour : 1 tbsp.
lemon : 1
carrot : 1
onion : 1
bay leaf
butter

Wash and scrub the mussels thoroughly. Put them in a large pot with the sliced up carrot, the onion, the chopped parsley, the bay and a little bit of the white wine. Heat through, the mussels will open. Stir them around sharply. Turn off the cooker once they have all opened.

Separately, fry the chopped shallots, and mix them with the white wine, a little of the water discharged by the mussels, a spoonful of flour and a knob of butter. Throw in the opened mussels. Taste the water and season if necessary.

Fried mussels

Easy ; 10 minutes.

Open the thoroughly cleaned mussels. Dry them. Detach the bodies from the shells and roll them one by one in flour. Then, straight into the pan with a little (not too much) hot oil !

Season with lemon and pepper. It's delicious.

Mussel brochettes

Rather long preparation-time ; 15 minutes.

Choose large, fat mussels. You'll need 4 lbs. for 4 people.

cut up salt pork : 7 oz.

or very very thin slices of bacon (ask your butcher to slice the meat, or else buy ready-sliced packets in a supermarket)

lemon : 2, cut into small pieces or else in halves for the juice

Open the mussels as in the "marinière" recipe. Take metal skewers, or else, best of all, sticks of rosemary or bay. Skewer the mussels.

Skewer each mussel with a piece of salt pork and a piece of lemon.

Or roll up the mussels in half slices of bacon, sprinkled with lemon.

Roll your prepared brochette in dried bread crumbs, then egg (or vice-versa).

Grill on a sheet of cast-iron, or else on the embers of a wood fire.

Mussel pilau

Cook the rice in the same water as the mussels ; Easy
>2 lbs. of mussels, 1 glass of rice, 2 tomatoes and 1 onion for
>2 people
>thyme, bay

Wash and scrub the mussels, then open them over heat. Keep the water. Fry together the tomatoes, onions, thyme and bay. Add the rice and stir for a minute or two. Pour on the water from the mussels and more boiling water. The volume of water must correspond to two and a half cups per cup of rice. Then add the open mussels, in their shells, and cook for 20 minutes. The water must completely disappear. You might add saffron, and if you have an adventurous soul, a little curry. Serve boiling hot.

Fishbread

Easy ; 1 hour.

This dish can be made with all sorts of fish or leftover fish that are mixed with the eggs and tomatoes ; but the best fishbread is made with monkfish or burbot. It is a true delight ; You will be asked whether it was crab or lobster !
>a 25 oz. monkfish, once entirely cleaned and scaled
>2 lbs.of seeded tomatoes, or 23 oz. of coulis
>6 eggs ; salt and pepper

Poach the fish for 5 minutes. Cut it into quite large pieces, about an inch square. Mix the eggs and tomatoes together, taking care that there isn't too much liquid. Mix the tomatoes and fish and check the seasoning. A little extra pepper won't do any harm. Put the preparation into a terrine. Cook in a double-boiler for 45 minutes.

You can check if it's cooked by piercing the fishbread with a sharp knife, it should remain clean. Serve cold, sliced or in the terrine with mayonnaise.

Red Mullet

Called "the woodcock of the seas".
A remarkable fish for its colour and very pronounced taste.
Favoured by the people of Provence, along with sea bass.

Grilled red mullet

Don't empty them.
Don't scale them.
Place the mullet on a grill or an oiled, very hot sheet of cast-iron.
Cook them delicately for 5 or 6 minutes on each side.
Remove the scales on your plate and savour the fish.
Provençal gourmets appreciate the mullet's insides and liver ;
others may find them too strong.

Red mullet "en papillote"

(cooked in tinfoil)
15 minutes ; very easy

    tinfoil or greaseproof paper
    a good large red mullet per person
    olive oil, salt, pepper, thyme

The mullet is to be scaled, you can empty it or not. The liver has a strong taste, which may not be to the taste of non-initiates.

Wrap the bright-eyed mullet in tinfoil, with some olive oil, salt, pepper and light-tasting thyme.

The sheet of tinfoil must be quite large and not touch the top of the fish. The same if you're using greaseproof paper. Bake for 10 minutes.

Red mullet in raw ham "papillotes"

red mullet : 1 nice one per person
raw ham : 1 thin slice per person
black olives : 20
bay, garlic, basil
parsley : 2 chopped tablespoonfuls
lemon : 2 spoonfuls

Mix the stoned and chopped olives with a clove of garlic, the parsley, basil and bay.

Empty the mullet. Place equal amounts of the black olive stuffing inside each fish. Envelop each one in a slice of ham with a bay leaf. Cook in a pre-heated oven for 15 or 20 minutes.

Thermostat 6 or 7.

I really like this slightly surprising recipe.

Sardines

Let us avoid speaking of the sardine that blocked the port of Marseilles, but look towards those bright, fresh and cheap sardines that are so happily presented by the region's fishmongers.

Deep-fried sardines

sardines : 3 or 4 per person
milk : a plateful
flour : a plateful
lemon : 1
olive oil, salt

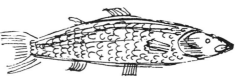

Wipe the sardines, scale them, but don't empty them.
Dip them in the milk and flour going from one plate to the next.
Throw them into boiling oil. Three minutes will be enough.
Sprinkle with salt and serve with a little lemon.

Sardine gratin with spinach

easy ; 30 minutes.

spinach : 2 lbs.
sardines : 1 or 2 per person
onion : 1
garlic, parsley, onion
milk : 5 tbsps.
nutmeg
flour : 1 spoonful

Blanch the spinach for 10 minutes, press and chop.

In an oiled pan, soften a chopped onion, add the spinach and stir for 3 minutes. Add chopped garlic and parsley, then the flour. Stir. Add the milk and a pinch of nutmeg and cook for 10 more minutes.

Scale and empty the sardines. Cut off their heads and remove their backbone. Lay them flat.

Put a little spinach (without juice) into each sardine. Roll them up, going from head to tail.

Push the sardines into the bed of spinach, placed in the bottom of a gratin dish. Place them tail up. Then pour the rest of the spinach over them so that the tails stick out.

Cover with dried bread crumbs and olive oil and cook for 10 minutes in the oven.

Sardine gratin with pine nuts

sardines : 2 lbs.

salted anchovies : 5 or 6

pine nuts : 5 oz.

parsley, bay, salt, pepper, olive oil and
1 lemon

Empty the sardines, decapitate them, remove the bones, scale and lay them flat. De-salt the anchovies, remove their backbone and soften them over heat until melted with olive oil, parsley and pine nuts.

Arrange the sardines in an oiled dish, stomachs upwards. Place the anchovies and pine nuts on top of them, then another layer of sardines, lying on their stomachs.

Sprinkle with lemon juice and a little olive oil. Finish with a layer of chapelure (dried bread crumbs), and cook in the oven for 10 to 20 minutes.

Variation : *Instead of laying them flat, roll up the sardines, tail-up.*

Sardine gratin with tomatoes

easy ; 1/2 an hour.

sardines : about 7 oz. per person

tomatoes : the same weight

onions, olive oil, parsley, garlic, salt, pepper

Scale and empty the sardines. Remove the heads and bones and lay flat. Peel and seed the tomatoes. In a gratin dish, alternate sardines, peeled and pressed tomatoes and herbs. Finish with dried bread crumbs and into the oven for ten minutes. Wipe the sardines thoroughly to be sure to remove all their scales.

"Sartagnade de poissons"

easy; 30 minutes.

From the name "sartan", meaning a frying pan. It consists of a mixture of deep-fried tiny fish : a "friture".

> 10 oz. of tiny fish
> olive oil, salt
> vinegar and lemon
> a deep frying pan

Dry thoroughly, and coat each fish in flour. Heat the oil in the pan, don't use too much. Drop the fish in the oil, so that they form a mass at the bottom. Let them cook without stirring, but shaking the pan. The fish will form a block. When they are nice and golden, turn them over and cook the other side. Serve them in a dish and pour into the pan a trickle of vinegar (2 tbsps.) which will be poured over the fish. One could also use lemon juice.

Tuna

Fresh tuna with tomatoes

easy; 30 minutes.

> tuna : 1 good slice
> tomatoes : 2 lbs.
> garlic, onion, parsley, thyme, salt, pepper

Fry the peeled tomatoes, sliced onion, thyme, bay and crushed garlic, as for a coulis. Add the slice of tuna and cook for a 1/2 hour.

Any slice of fish can be cooked in this way. But you can also brown the fish in another pan and add it at the last minute to the tomato sauce.

Good woman's tunafish ("à la bonne femme")

Easy ; 30 minutes.

> tuna : a good slice, over an inch thick
> onions : 1 or 2
> white wine : 1 glass
> vinegar : 1/2 glass
> garlic : 2 cloves
> flour : 1 spoonful
> tomato coulis
> parsley
> olive oil
> salt, pepper

Blanch the slice of tunafish for 5 minutes, drain it and put it in the pan with the olive oil. Brown both sides and remove it from the pan.

Fry the chopped onions with a spoonful of flour, the white wine, vinegar, crushed garlic and a spoonful of coulis. Put the tuna back in the pan. Cook on low heat for 20 minutes, covered.

Serve with chopped parsley and steamed potatoes.

Chartreuse of tunafish

> one thick slice of tuna
> two to four pounds of onions
> three or four lemons
> four or five tomatoes
> four or five carrots
> lots of lettuce : two, three or more
> salt, pepper, olive oil

Use a large casserole. At the bottom, place a layer of onions about two fingers deep, then a layer of tomatoes and the broken up lettuce. Don't hesitate to use a lot. Add the lemons and carrots cut into rounds and place the slice of tuna on top (with or without its skin). Then continue the succession of layers.

Moisten with a glass or two of olive oil and cook on low heat for two or three hours. Everything should have melted together, everything will be delicious.

Add a small glass of Green Chartreuse, during the cooking.

Also, see "Fish soups", in the Soup chapter

Special advice on fish :

To grill your fish, envelop them, without scaling them beforehand, with cooking salt. The salt will form a shell, and keep the flesh tender.

The scales will come off with the salt.

Meat

Provence, lacking in pastures, is especially reputed for its lamb. In winter they graze the fine herbs of the garrigues and in summer, the sweet grass of the Alpine pastures. Their scented flesh needs no sauce and is good grilled, roasted in the oven, or on a spit. The wood for the fire used to be chosen particularly, almond tree, oak or juniper, their embers embalming the flesh with different flavours. Today, sheets of cast-iron and the oven have replaced the wood-fire. It may not be quite as good, but is far more practical. Pork in Haute Provence is still excellent. It is not demeaning to eat pork, considered elsewhere to be a poor-man's meat. It is most often cooked with sage. As for beef, it is best to cook it for a long time.

Nothing could be more famous than The Daube.

To each family their own recipe, and each daube will be different from the last

The last one I ate had been cooking for two days, in the corner of the fireplace. Not to be equalled, supreme, ephemeral, I could never describe it, but here is the recipe.

It wasn't cooked in the "daubière", a varnished pottery dish with a rounded handle and a hollow lid into which water is poured during the cooking, but in a cast-iron pot, on a tripod.

Here is Christiane's recipe for :

The Daube

Easy, but long cooking-time.

> meat : topside or eye, or topside and eye : 4 lbs.
> onions : 2
> garlic : 2 cloves
> carrots : 3
> strong red wine : 1 3/4 pts.
> a little vinegar
> salt, pepper
> bacon fat : 6 oz.
> bouquet garni : 2
> bay
> a little dried orange peel
> a tiny pinch of nutmeg
> 2 cloves
> 4 crushed juniper berries

Leave the meat, cut into square pieces (about an inch and a half square), to marinate for five or six hours in the red wine with a spoonful of vinegar, the two quartered onions, three chopped carrots and the herbs, except for the garlic and dried orange peel.

Then, put the chopped bacon fat to melt in the bottom of the daubière, or stewing pot. Remove the scum with a skimmer. Brown a quartered onion. Add the meat and garnish, after having drained it. Brown for a minute.

Add two cloves of garlic and the piece of dried orange peel and humidify with the marinade. Stir well.

Add a pint of warm water and another bouquet garni.

Cover with the daubière lid, filled with water, or else simply with the cooking pot lid.

Cook for four hours or more.

One can now find new cast-iron pots with wonderful lids. Their inside is studded with tiny bumps that guide the steam skilfully over the meat.

Daube is served accompanied with steamed potatoes, a macaronade or fresh pasta.

Macaronade : *Half-cooked macaroni, watered with the daube cooking juices and cooked au gratin in the oven with Gruyère and dried bread crumbs.*

This is a truly traditional recipe for daube ; "the real thing". Many people won't stand for any other. All the same, here are two others that I think are both excellent :

One from Avignon, with lamb.

And one from Lourmarin, without wine.

Avignon daube

a chopped shoulder of lamb
7 oz. of chopped bacon fat
2 onions
2 carrots
parsley, 2 cloves of crushed garlic
bay, a sprig of rosemary
1 clove, nutmeg, pepper, salt
16 fl. oz. of white wine
8 fl. oz. of olive oil

Leave the ingredients and meat to soak with the white wine.

Melt the fat in a casserole with an onion. Brown the chopped meat, then add the marinade (sieved or not).

Cook for two and a half to three hours and serve with steamed potatoes.

Lourmarin daube

without wine.

a variety of meat :
rump : 1 lb.
topside : 1 lb.
chuck : 1 lb.
olive oil : 2 tbsps. per person
good wine vinegar : 1 tsp. per person
garlic : 2 cloves
1 onion
1 walnut per person
a piece of dried orange peel
bay, parsley, two cloves, salt and pepper

Prepare the marinade a day in advance :

Very finely chopped garlic and onion, and pound all the ingredients together with the oil and vinegar. Beat thoroughly with a whisk, this should produce a paste. Cover the meat with this mixture, make sure it is completely coated and leave it overnight, covered, in a cool place.

The next day, pour the meat and marinade into a casserole, cover and cook for four or five hours.

Skim off the fat, serve on heated plates.

Variation : *This stew may also be served with halved walnuts added midway through the cooking time with a sugarlump to remove the acidity of the vinegar.*

Wild boar daube

Bred or wild boar meat is very good cooked in stew.

     a 4 to 6 pound haunch
     a pint of dry white wine
     a glass of water
     4 cloves of garlic
     3 chopped shallots
     cloves, bay, salt, peppercorns
     10 crushed juniper berries

A day in advance, cut the haunch into inch square pieces and put it in the marinade (white wine, water, ingredients) with 4 juniper berries.

The next day, pour the whole thing into a covered casserole and simmer for five hours.

Five minutes before the end of the cooking-time, add six crushed juniper berries.

Serve the stew boiling hot with steamed potatoes.

Provençal Pot-au-feu

A very hearty dish, to be made for a large number of guests.

Meat (at least three different sorts) :

beef : short rib : 3 lbs.

lamb : shin : 1 lb. (the lower part of the leg with the bone)

1 chicken

3 sausages

a marrow bone

There must be at least three times as much beef as there is lamb.

Stock :

garlic : 4 unpeeled cloves

onions : 3

2 cloves

leeks : 2

celery : 2 leaves

bay, thyme, chervil

salt, pepper

Vegetables :

turnips : 3

leeks : 1 small bunch

carrots : 7 or 8

celery : 2 hearts

Put the different pieces of meat into six pints of cold water in a large pot. Bring to the boil. Skim more than once. Stop the boiling and simmer. Put in the stock and vegetables. Add salt and whole peppercorns. Cook for three hours. Also, prepare the accompanying vegetables, tying them into small bunches with string. Hang the ends of the strings over the side of the pot, you will find it easier to take out the vegetables when the time comes. Add these vegetables an hour after you brought the meat to a simmer.

Serve in warm plates, with cooking salt, mustard, pickles, little onions and even some tomato coulis.

The marrow bone should be wrapped in gauze to prevent the marrow escaping. It will be served on croutons.

The meat could also be served accompanied with a hot or cold chickpea salad.

Beef with basil

A lot like Carpaccio, so easy to make and deliciously fresh tasting !

beef fillet : about 7 oz. per person
(or else rumpsteak ; much cheaper...)
basil : a small handful
lemons : 2 or 3
olive oil
3 spoonfuls of capers

Put the piece of meat in the freezer for an hour. Then do your best to cut the meat into very thin slices. Place them on individual plates or in a large flat plate, with some tender salad leaves. Four slices per person. Pour the sauce, made from 10 spoonfuls of olive oil, the chopped basil and the juice from the three lemons, over the meat. Sprinkle with capers. Then chill for an hour in the fridge and serve.

It will be delicious on a summer evening.

(You could also ask your butcher to cut the very thin slices...)

Veal with aubergines

tendron of veal : 2 lbs.

aubergines : 10

olive oil, salt, pepper

Brown the meat in olive oil. Add the pieces of chopped, peeled and blanched aubergine. Simmer for an hour and a half in a casserole. One can add tomatoes, to make the dish a little less dry.

Beefsteak with anchovy and tomato

beefsteak : piece of your choice

anchovy : 2 fillets per person

tomato : 1 per person

pepper, butter or oil

De-salt the anchovies and remove their bones. Pound them down to a thick paste.

Cook the halved tomatoes in a pan for 5 minutes and keep them warm.

Grill the steak, to each person's taste, without salt. Serve the meat with the anchovies spread over the top, and the tomatoes on top or on the side.

You can use anchovy paste in a tube. It'll be less authentic, but so much easier !

Pork

Usually accompanied with sage leaves.
The not-too-fat loin will be less dry than the fillet.

Roast pork with sage

1 hour.

pork loin : 2 lbs.

sage : 20 dried leaves

garlic : 10 cloves

Ask your butcher for a pork loin. Do not have it boned, but ask him to stab the piece between each rib. Once it has been cooked, it will be easier to cut. Pound the sage leaves and garlic in a mortar.

Make slits in the meat, slip the mixture into them. Brush the meat with the rest of the mixture and a few crushed peppercorns. Put the roast into a very hot oven, or cook it in a casserole, checking it often. If needs be, add a little stock.

Boiled roast pork with vegetables.

pork : 1 deboned fillet, 40 to 60 oz., plus the bones.

carrots, turnips, onions studded with cloves, celery

salt, pepper, bay, sage

Put the carefully bound pork in cold water with the bones. Boil slowly. Remove the scum once, then again. Remove the bones and add the vegetables. Boil for an hour then leave to cool. Cut into slices.

Serve with a salad containing some lettuce and the vegetables that were cooked with the pork. Mustard. Pickles.

Pork cutlets

From the fillet, or from the loin.

Cook them slowly in a pan, with olive oil. Sprinkle with sage leaves. They can be cooked covered with a little water to make them more tender, after they have browned.

Variation : Add tomatoes, already cooked or not. Also add peppers. Cook everything together on not too high heat for 15 minutes.

Pork fillet
(to be served cold)

I try to choose a fillet that will produce attractive slices.

> pork : approx. 2 pounds and a half, plus the bones
> garlic : 3 crushed cloves
> olive oil : 3 tbsps.
> sage : 20 leaves
> salt, crushed peppercorns

Ask your butcher to place a mixture of sage and pepper inside the roast before tying it. Bring this yourself if he doesn't have it ready prepared.

Heat thoroughly a casserole containing olive oil, garlic and the bones. Put the roast in and brown it thoroughly on all sides. Remove the bones and roast. Pour in a glass of warm water while scraping the bottom of the pot, then add the sage leaves. Put the roast back and place two or three leaves on the meat. Cover and cook on a low flame for two hours. There must be no water left when the cooking is finished.

If using a pressure cooker, cooking-time will be 20 minutes.

Lamb

Grilled lamb

The best are of course done on the coals of a wood fire. Beware of forest fires ! How many hectares have burnt for a cutlet !

The grill on which the meat is placed must be at least 4 inches above the coals. For those who like the meat black and burnt, an inch will be enough.

If you don't have a small barbecue, cook on a lightly oiled cast-iron sheet that has been well heated beforehand.

A rotisserie is ideal for leg of lamb.

I like to rub the meat to be grilled with thyme and a little olive oil.

Take care ! if you are also using leaves of savory, these have the inconvenience of being very sharp and will prick the throat disagreeably. Crush them to avoid any eventual panic and suffocation !

Grilled cutlets on the bone

Provide more than one per person.

Whatever you do, do not buy any for guests or family who don't like grilled fat and who will scornfully leave it on the side of their plate. Apart from not knowing what's good for them, their appetite will remain unsatisfied since there is only a small eye of meat to be had on these cutlets.

Double cutlets present the same problem though the meat is more abundant.

It is best therefore, to forget about the price and get some good slices of saddle or leg, they will be delicious and plentiful.

Brochettes

Brochettes made with a branch of rosemary or bay will be very flavourful.

Brochettes of shoulder of lamb alternating (or not) with kidneys or liver are absolutely delicious.

Before browning them, pass them lightly through a plate of olive oil and herbs. Salt after cooking (5 to 10 minutes).

Bay accompanies meat cooked "en brochette" particularly well.

Roast shoulder of lamb

Choose a three pound shoulder, smaller if there are only two of you.

Ask your butcher to detach the meat from the flat bone (I think it's the shoulder blade...), but not to remove it. If you were to remove it the meat will curl up during the cooking. When carving, the bone will be more easily removed, and the slices will be larger.

Cook it like a leg of lamb, thoroughly rubbed with oil and herbs. 20 minutes per pound.

Serve it with a ratatouille, or else aubergines and tomato. It will be delicious.

Otherwise, cooked on a bed of potatoes like a "gigot boulangère", it will make an exquisite dish.

Leg of lamb and garlic cream

Only leg of lamb is eaten now. Choose it well rounded. Around the Easter period they are delicious and the butchers are rapidly cleaned out.

Frozen lamb isn't bad either.

Cooking-time : 20 minutes per pound.

olive oil, thyme

and for the garlic cream :

a good twenty cloves of garlic.

The leg : rub it thoroughly with thyme-flavoured olive oil. I also rub it with a halved-lemon which will ad to the crispiness of the skin (I also do this for roast fowl).

Some people recommend that the meat be slivered with garlic. Others on the contrary do not like it, but will arrange in the dish, whole cloves (crushed in their skin) around the meat. Their flavour will flavour the meat (unless they burn).

Put the meat into a very hot oven, pre-heated 15 minutes. The lamb will thus be thoroughly seized.

When the lamb is done, according to the cook's taste, carve it well. This is important so as to get the most slices possible out of it, and it's also important because well-carved meat is better.

One does have to sit, in forced silence, through some real carving-massacres.

Serve it with a garlic cream, made on the side.

Those who like garlic use the cream abundantly, while those who don't ignore it to the profit of the former.

Cook 20 unpeeled cloves of garlic in water. Change the water once. Stop the cooking when the garlic softens. Pinch them and the clove will come out. Reduce them to a paste, add salt, pepper and, if needs be, a little cooking water. The cream mustn't be too watery.

"Gigot boulangère"

leg of lamb : not more than three pounds
potatoes : 2 per person
tomatoes : 2
garlic : 3 cloves
onions : 2
thyme, bay, pepper, salt, olive oil

Cut the potatoes into thin slices and arrange them in a well-oiled gratin dish, with slices of peeled tomato and onion rings. Slip in the unpeeled, crushed garlic. Mix it all together and flatten it carefully. Cook for ten minutes in a hot oven (salt, pepper).

Then place the leg of lamb in the dish or on the grill, on the dish (I prefer it that way since the meat cooks better).

Cook everything together, watching over the cooking. Be careful that the potatoes don't shrivel up. If this happens, add a little water.

Serve everything together, very hot.

Don't fight too much over who gets to scrape the bottom of the dish.

Pieds - z - et - Paquets "

(literally "Feet and Packets")

Everyone loves this from Marseilles to Sisteron. You must like tripe, this is an unavoidable condition. Eat them boiling hot, on hot plates.

Various possibilities :

Open a tin or jar of delicious pieds-et-paquets (Choose the brand carefully).
Serve them boiling hot with steamed potatoes.

Buy ready-made pieds-et-paquets at your butcher's. Prepare and cook them in the sauce. But they have usually beeen stuffed which is too bad.

After having scalded them, put them into the sauce and white wine (see next recipe) and cook them for two hours in a pressure-cooker or for eight to ten hours in a normal pot.

Make them yourself; this will take quite a long time... So invite friends, prepare them together and have some fun.

Order stomachs and feet from your butcher. Wash them carefully, wipe them dry and cut the stomachs into four-inch squares.

For 6 people :

> tripe, that is to say stomach : 3 lbs.
> feet : 6
> lean bacon : 12 oz.
> 1 onion, 1 carrot, lots of parsley
> 3 garlic cloves
> tomatoes : 2 lbs.
> white wine : 1 glass per pound
> pepper

Place on each square a spoonful of stuffing (that is to say chopped parsley, a little garlic, lots of pepper) and a piece of bacon. You will have made a "buttonhole" with a knife in a corner of the square. Fold over and get the packet to close starting with the side opposite to the "buttonhole"!... The packet must be perfectly closed. It's difficult to explain.

Sweat the packets for 3 minutes in a pot without any fat, stirring constantly. Then drain them. After this operation the packets should hold together a lot better.

The sauce or broth : Soften in three spoonfuls of olive oil, the finely chopped onion and two carrots, the peeled tomatoes, three cloves of garlic, along with the white wine.

Feet-and-Packets : Fry them for 15 minutes, stirring.

Arrange in the bottom of a casserole : 3 feet (or half the number of feet that you are using), then the drained packets, then the 3 other feet. Cover with the sauce.

Cook for 2 hours in a pressure cooker, or 8 to 10 hours in a casserole. Serve the "Feet-and-Packets" boiling hot on very hot plates, with steamed potatoes. You can put the sauce through a vegetable mill, it will be creamier.

Fowl, Rabbit, Game and Snails

If you own a spit, choose that method of cooking over all others, it being the best for a young bird, tender and plump.

Don't bard your bird, moisten and salt it halfway through the cooking.

If you want a nice and crispy bird, rub it with a mixture of olive oil and lemon (The skin must be rubbed with a halved lemon). A little cayenne pepper can be added.

If you don't have a spit, put your bird in the oven — always very hot, pre-heated 15 minutes — on the grill, with a little water in the dripping-pan.

Think of putting a dish of vegetables, potatoes, half-cooked mushrooms, under the bird. These will catch the juices.

Another cooking method : in a tinfoil or grease-proof paper envelope. The pieces mustn't be too big. Salt is added afterwards. The meat can be covered with herbs. The "papillotes" (envelopes made out of tinfoil or paper) present the advantage of keeping the oven clean, and of thus not perfuming the whole house, or whole building, with your meal.

Watch out for rabbit bones, sharp and pointed. Never give them to your favorite animals, except for goldfish and canaries...

If you are carving the rabbit try to keep the bones clear to avoid them breaking and creating sharp ends.

Did you know that rabbit must not be eaten on boats, whether sailing or rowing ? ! It brings bad luck... but I don't know why.

Chicken

Choose a good farm chicken which may be a little expensive but also much better and won't be stringy.

Chicken with garlic

A terrine, a chicken
garlic : a lot : 50 cloves !
croutons of bread, olive oil, salt, pepper

Once your chicken has been prepared and filled with unpeeled and crushed garlic, put it into an oiled casserole or terrine dish.

You will have inserted a crouton rubbed with garlic to block the rump opening, and another smaller one in the neck. Salt and pepper the insides of the chicken. Surround the chicken with cloves of garlic. Close the terrine or casserole, and cook for an hour in the oven, without lifting up the lid, after having poured a little stock or salted water in the pot.

Open the casserole or terrine in the middle of the table in front of your guests.

The marvelous smell of the garlic (or of the oil !) will delight everyone in advance. Each diner can crush the garlic on his croutons.

Chicken fricassee with garlic

1 chicken or 2
garlic : 10 unpeeled cloves
bouquet garni
bacon : 5 oz.
dry white wine : 7 fl. oz.
salt, pepper, olive oil

Brown the pieces of chicken in an oiled and deep frying pan, add the bouquet garni, 8 cloves of garlic. Cover and cook gently for 20 minutes. Remove the pieces of chicken.

During this time, cook rapidly the chopped bacon and chicken livers, put them through the blender with the 8 pressed cloves of garlic. Spread this paste on slices of toasted bread.

Place these slices at the bottom of the pan — from which the fat will have been removed with the white wine.

Place the pieces of cooked chicken on the slices of bread, and cook on high heat. Serve with chopped parsley and garlic.

Chicken stuffed with juniper

chicken : 1

stuffing :

    6 juniper berries

    5 oz. of (leftover) pork

    5 oz. of (leftover) veal

    sheep brains

    egg : 1 set

    sage, bay, garlic

    salt, pepper, olive oil

Prepare the stuffing with the crushed and pounded juniper, chopped meat, brain, chicken liver. Bind with the egg. Add salt, pepper.

Insert the stuffing into the chicken, with the crushed but not peeled clove of garlic. Block the openings with a crouton of bread, or sew up the chicken.

Cook it slowly in an oiled casserole, or else in the oven. Baste it often during the cooking : about an hour.

Chicken with olives

one cut-up chicken
salt pork
two cloves of garlic
one shallot
a glass of white wine
a handful of black olives
bouquet garni, thyme, bay
olive oil, salt, pepper

Fry the salt pork and remove it. Thoroughly brown the pieces of chicken and remove them. Fry the shallot, pour in the glass of white wine, add the bouquet garni, bay, chopped garlic, salt and pepper. Cook, uncovered, for ten minutes. Put the pieces of chicken and salt pork back in the pan. Finish by adding the black olives, stoned or not (I find the stones add taste). Check the cooking and serve with boiled potatoes, pasta or rice, Provençal tomatoes or ratatouille...

Chicken with Pastis

for 6 hungry people :

2 chickens
olive oil : 8 fl. oz.
tomatoes : 6
fennel branch
slices of bread : 5
onions : 2
Pastis : 1 glass
garlic : 6 cloves
parsley : 1 large bunch
potatoes : 4
chilli peppers : 1 or 2
saffron : 2 little boxes of filaments, if possible
salt, pepper

The day before — or three hours in advance, if you're in a hurry — cut up the chicken, marinate it in a terrine with the saffron, a little salt, pepper, the pastis, and a glass of olive oil.

In the casserole, soften together the onions, garlic, peeled and chopped tomatoes, stirring all the while. Then place the fennel branches, the parsley, the chicken. Cover with the marinade and boiling water. Boil for ten minutes, covered. Add the potatoes cut into thick rounds and simmer for twenty minutes, still covered. Then, at the last minute, bring it rapidly back to the boil for a few seconds so that the oil mixes in well.

Before serving on slices of stale bread, add a little more saffron.

Pound together in a mortar, one clove of garlic, the chicken liver, two chilli peppers, moisten with some hot broth. Add two or three slices of cooked potato and crush everything together.

Chicken with pastis is usually very much appreciated. Feel free to make a lot. It is also good re-heated, and keeps well in the freezer.

Chicken with thyme "en paquetoun"

1 young chicken
sliced smoked bacon
thyme, olive oil, salt, pepper

Cut up the raw chicken. Roll the pieces in thyme, pressing down hard. Wrap the pieces in slices of smoked bacon. Truss and put the pieces in a dish, in the oven, under the grill.

Cook for 20 minutes. Close the oven for ten minutes so that the pieces swell up. Serve with a salad and chips.

Same preparation for rabbit

Truffled and roasted chicken

1 chicken
truffles : 2 or 3
pork fat
salt, pepper

Prepare it a day or two in advance so that the truffle flavour impregnates the chicken completely. The sliced truffles are to be placed under the skin. Pound the truffle peelings in a mortar with the chicken liver, salt, pepper and a little pork fat. Then mix with the rest of the truffles cut into larger pieces. Garnish the inside of the chicken and bard it. Cook it in a casserole, or on a spit.

Chicken salad

leftover chicken
tomatoes, avocados

Mix the pieces of chicken with a good tomato and avocado salad. Season generously with mustard and cream.

Taste it.

"Poule au pot" with saffron

hen : 1
tomatoes : 5
onions : 2
cloves of garlic : 15

bouquet garni, white wine, water, salt, pepper, saffron

Cook the hen with the onions, tomatoes, unpeeled garlic, bouquet garni, wine and water in a casserole for an hour and a half. Season very generously. Serve with rice cooked in the broth (3 glasses of broth for every glass of rice). Add a pinch of saffron in the rice.

Guinea-fowl with figs

I like this recipe, it tastes of seasons and autumn.

> guinea-fowl : 2
>
> dry white wine : 1 large glass
>
> figs : 2 lbs. of fresh figs
>
> water : 1 glass
>
> salt, pepper, olive oil with a knob of butter

Empty the guinea-fowl, cut a pound of figs in two. Fry the guinea fowl in a casserole. Toss in the butter and oil. Put the birds back in, with the halved figs all around them.

Add salt and pepper. Then add the wine and water. Cover and cook for 40 minutes. Add the rest of the figs (whole). Cook for 15 minutes.

To serve, put the liquid through a vegetable mill and pour it into the serving dish with some creole rice.

(If you are in a hurry you can put all the figs in at the same time) This is delicious and surprising !

Thrush

One cannot buy thrush any longer. I am glad for the birds, but sorry for us !... Everyone has a fond memory of the "rôties", cooked in the fireplace, with a piece of bread.

If you come from a family of hunters, you won't need a recipe.

And if you have no thrush...

Quails au gratin

quails : 1 or 2 per person, bards of bacon

potatoes : 1 lb.

milk, cream, juniper, olive oil, salt, pepper

Place a not too thick layer of sliced potatoes in an oiled tian. Add salt and pepper. And again. Bathe in cream and milk. Cook in the oven until the milk is completely absorbed.

Arrange your barded quails in the tian with three crushed juniper berries, inside and on top. Bake in the hot oven for 15 minutes. Serve hot with a gratin.

Christmas turkey

For the 25th of december.

Cook it on a spit in the chimney, or else in the oven.

one young and not too fat turkey

10 oz. of raw ham and sausage meat

1 onion

1 fennel branch

2 pounds of chestnuts with their shells

1 or more truffles

salt, pepper, olive oil

Cut the truffles into very thin slices a day in advance, and insert them between skin and flesh.

The next day, cook the chestnuts in their skins, in salt water flavoured with a twig of fennel. Peel them once they've cooked. Separate them into two equal piles.

Prepare the stuffing with half the chestnuts, the browned onion, the ham and sausage meat in little pieces and the chopped turkey liver. Add pepper, simmer for ten minutes. To make the stuffing less dry, you could add three "Petits Suisses" (about 3 oz. cream cheese).

Stuff the turkey. Sow up the opening and put it in a hot oven, with the rest of the chestnuts around it.

As soon as it has gone golden brown place a sheet of tinfoil over it. Baste it often. Allow twenty minutes per pound cooking time.

Rabbit

You can recognize a fresh rabbit by its smooth liver. Be careful with its sharp bones. Never give them to eat to animals like dogs or cats.

Rabbit with garlic

rabbit : 1 or 2 cut up young ones
garlic : 23 cloves
white wine : 31/2 fl. oz.
salt, pepper, olive oil
parsley : a very big bunch
Cognac : 1 liqueur glass

Brown the pieces of rabbit in a little olive oil, on medium heat. Flambé with the Cognac, add salt and pepper.

Add the white wine, the peeled garlic (whole), and the parsley.

Let simmer for 25 to 30 minutes.

Serve with fresh pasta or steamed potatoes.

Sprinkle with parsley.

Rabbit with fennel

rabbit : 1, cut up
fennel : 6 bulbs
garlic : 2 cloves, bouquet garni
onions : 3
white wine : 16 fl. oz.
flour or cornflour
salt, pepper, olive oil

Fry the pieces of rabbit in a casserole with the olive oil. Brown them well. Add the sliced onions and the garlic, the white wine and the bouquet garni. Simmer for 30 minutes. Add the halved fennel bulbs. Cook for 15 minutes.

To serve, bind the sauce with a little cornflour, or flour. Pour it over the rabbit and fennel. The sauce should be plentiful.

Rabbit with juniper

Marinate the pieces of rabbit with olive oil and crushed juniper for 24 hours.

Wrap the pieces of rabbit with a slice of bacon, with a little thyme. Tie with string and arrange the pieces in an oiled tian. Into the oven. Check that it isn't too dry. A little broth can be added. Allow 45 to 60 minutes cooking-time and serve hot.

Rabbit with herbs

very young rabbit
thyme, bay, savory
rosemary, garlic crushed into a paste
olive oil, salt, white wine, mustard

Marinate the rabbit with the herbs in a covered dish for twenty four hours.

The next day, place thyme and savory (careful with the sharp leaves) in the rabbit's stomach. Then spread mustard over the rabbit, pour olive oil over it and put it in the oven.

Add salt half way through the cooking. Allow 3/4 of an hour to an hour, more or less. Serve very hot.

Rabbit with olives

1 rabbit and some salted pork (a 3 oz. slice)

2 onions

2 lbs. of tomatoes

1 handful of de-salted green olives

garlic, mother-of-thyme (wild thyme), thyme, bay, pepper, olive oil

Put the cut up rabbit into a marinade of olive oil, thyme, mother-of-thyme, bay and pepper two or three hours before you begin cooking. Fry the pieces with the salted pork. Add the tomatoes, onions, herbs and crushed garlic. Pour in the olives and cook slowly for an hour.

Rabbit with thyme "en paquetoun"

Same recipe as for chicken.

Rabbit in poor-man's sauce

rabbit : 1

mustard, onion, flour, vinegar

Roast the rabbit and its liver for 15 minutes. Remove the liver. Chop it up and fry it with an onion.

Add a little flour and water with a trickle of vinegar. Put it through the blender.

The rabbit is cooked on its own in a casserole. Serve it with the sauce.

This recipe can also be made with the rabbit cut in pieces. Serve with fresh pasta.

Wild boar

Common in Haute-Provence, both bred and wild. It produces nice meat, roast, or in stew.

Wild boar stew

4 to 6 pounds of shoulder
10 ounces of salt pork

marinade :

1 3/4 pints of red wine
2 sliced onions
1/2 pound of carrots
juniper, savory, thyme, bay
1 spoonful of wine vinegar
parsley, cooking salt and peppercorns

Cook this marinade for 15 minutes and leave it to cool off. Put in the pieces of wild boar. Leave the meat for 4 or 5 days in the marinade, in a cool place. Fry the salt pork in the daubière, and the pieces of meat. Brown very thoroughly and remove. Put some bacon rind in the bottom of the stewing pot with the olive oil and add the pieces of boar. Cover with marinade. Put on low heat, with some water in the lid of the daubière as soon as it boils. Three quarters of the way through the cooking add two spoonfuls of Eau-de-vie. Boil for five minutes and cover it quickly. Cook for at least three hours, sometimes five hours !... Serve it boiling hot. You could add three or four juniper berries at the last minute, and crush a few walnuts into it.

Very good re-heated, keeps well in the freezer.

If the sauce is too watery, I bind it with a little flour.

 Snails

There couldn't be a book of Provençal cooking that didn't speak of snails. But if someone talks to you of "limaçoun", you should know that these aren't little slugs ("limaces"), but small white snails, with black spiralled stripes.

They are to be found at the end of the summer, congregating at the top of fennel plants (from which comes their Provençal name "escalo fenoum").

Do not get the bright idea of making an original bouquet with the plants, or first of all your car, then your house will be striped with shining paths showing that their persistent immobility on the fennel was but a wait for the great move !

But what a pleasure it is to eat them in Marseilles.

The Marseilles shopkeepers will propose them to you cooked in water with lots of herbs and spices. They hold out their cornets of "limaçoun" and wet the appetite with their accent : "a l'aigo sau le limaçoun / y en a des gros et des pitchoun !"

Buy one of their paper cornets and treat yourself to something special.

If you are told about "petits gris" ("little greys "), you should know that they are neither small nor grey , but quite big and brown.

They are our garden snails who gorge themselves on our lettuces and seedlings.

It is forbidden to collect them before the month of June, because of the breeding season.

"Petits gris" snails in sauce

Collect them and starve them for up to a fortnight in an aired receptacle. The last few days, give them little branches of thyme and powder them with flour.

Then throw them into a large basin of warm water. Remove their capsule and check that they are all alive. Then put them in a large basin with two glasses of olive oil and a large handful of salt. Stir. They will disgorge their slime. Wait for a while and rince, rince, rince and rince again... until the water stays clear.

You will need :

> coriander seeds, one orange peel, garlic, peppercorns, a little rosemary, thyme, bay, basil and mint, three leeks, two turnips, three carrots and some celery branches.

Once they have been thoroughly rinsed, put the snails in a pot of unsalted, cold water. Heat it more and more. The snails' horns will appear, then bring to the boil suddenly. Remove the scum and add lots of salt. Cook for an hour and a half with all the ingredients except for the mint, then for another hour with the vegetables, until the snails can be detached from their shells with a pin.

During this time, prepare the sauce ; you will need :

> six or seven anchovies, a glass of white wine, two slices of diced raw ham, a branch of fennel, an onion, a small orange peel, three tomatoes, some parsley, six cloves of garlic, a little flour and some vinegar.

Soften the anchovies with the vinegar until melted. Add the white wine, ham, ingredients, flour, crushed garlic, with a little flavoured cooking water.

Take the snails out from their water, drain them, and pour them into the sauce, with or without their shells. The sauce shouldn't be watery, but must also cover the snails. Leave it to simmer for about an hour.

Some people like to add a bowl of crushed walnuts at the last minute.

#

Provençal goat cheeses have the highest reputation. To each his own, soft, fresh or hard.

Look out for the so-called Banon cheese that is made in the Isère or in the Drôme. The best ones come from Banon, near Forcalquier, and its area. They are called "pliés" ("folded"). To fold in Provençal means to wrap something. They are indeed wrapped in chestnut leaves.

And have you never heard the salesgirl, in a grocer's or elsewhere, proposing to wrap a bottle of wine or a lampshade, asking : "voulez-vous que je vous le plie ?" ("shall I fold it for you ?") ? !

Cachaye

Crush a fresh tomme. Pepper it and pour eau-de-vie over it. Mix well and place in a cool place. It is ready to eat when the cheese tastes spicy. In the Gavot country, it is kept for the whole winter and then, it is very difficult for the non-initiated palate to keep from grimacing !

Goat cheese in oil

Take some not-too-fresh cheeses (fresh cheeses would disintegrate) and place them in a jar. Surround them with savory (branches and leaves), one or two bay leaves, and pour light olive oil over them, to cover. Wait for a month.

You can sprinkle your salads with pieces of these cheeses and olives. A treat...

Puddings

Critics of Provençal cooking do not believe there are any. It is true that the Provençal puddings cannot rival with the cream tarts, meringues and chocolates of their neighbors.

They are rustic puddings, based on honey, almonds, fritters that end a meal, simple sweets.

Chichi-Fregi

Famous in Marseilles. No child could forget them from the votive feasts of Provence. Just the name is an enchantment !

flour : 1 lb.
baker's yeast : 1/2 packet
salt : a pinch
orange-blossom water : 2 tbsps.
warm water
vanilla-flavoured sugar

Mix the yeast with warm water.
Mix it with the flour, the salt, the orange-blossom water, and add

warm water until it has the consistency of a flexible dough. Leave it to rest for an hour under a cloth.

Into hot oil, a ribbon of dough is poured in a large spiral, which is then cut with scissors when cooked. It is then rolled in sugar.

Marvels or oreillettes

(or "bugnes des Lyonnais")

They appear at Carnaval time.

> flour : 1 lb.
> eggs : 4
> orange-blossom water : 1 spoonful (or lime-blossom)
> sugar : 1 spoonful
> icing sugar
> butter : 1/2 pound
> or oil : 3 tbsps.
> yeast : 1/2 packet

Mix everything together. If it seems too dry, add a little warm water. Make a ball. Leave it for two hours under a cloth in a warm place. Spread it out with a pastry roller, very, very, very flat.

Cut it into long strips with a pastry-cutter or a knife. Split or twist them. Toss them into hot deep-frying oil. Take them out and place them on paper towel. Sprinkle with icing sugar.

For the traditional Christmas Eve **Thirteen Desserts** ; see the chapter devoted to the "Gros souper"

Pan Coudoun

> quinces : 1 per person
> bread dough

Choose the quinces small and ripe. Wipe them off, empty the

middles, fill them with sugar or jam, a little butter and lemon or honey. Spread out the dough. Wrap each quince in it. Gild it with egg. Bake in a hot oven, 30 or 40 minutes !

A delicious smell will permeate your home, and your neighbors will probably pay you a — surprise — visit !

Sweet spinach tart

A speciality of the Vaucluse, particularly Carpentras

sablé pastry
spinach : 1 lb.
milk : 16 fl. oz.
sugar : 3 oz.
flour : 2 spoonfuls
eggs : 4
lemon : 1
cristallized fruit : mixed cherries and oranges

Spread the pastry out in a tart mould (save some strips). Blanch the spinach for 2 minutes and press it to drain. Chop it as finely as possible. Beat the eggs with the flour and sugar. Mix them with boiling hot milk, the spinach, a piece of lemon peel and the little pieces of cristallized fruit. Place this over the pastry and arrange the rest of the pastry cut into strips in a criss-cross on top. Decorate each square with a cristallized cherry.

Cook in a hot oven for ten minutes or a medium oven for thirty minutes.

Instead of cristallized fruit, you could use Smyrna raisins dipped in warm rum. You might also add pine nuts.

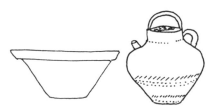

" *Le Gros Souper* "

This the Christmas eve supper, on the evening of the 24th of December. In Provence, it is the most important meal of the year. A meatless but sumptuous meal (where one recognizes the skilfulness of the Provençal cook), that the whole family attends, forgetting all quarrels. A communion in food, charged with pagan and religious symbols.

The "Big supper" used to be preceded with the ceremony of the "cacho fuo", where the oldest member of the family would carefully choose a branch from a fruit tree (often almond) and pour wine over it. The youngest would then light it in the fireplace, using a piece of wood from last year's log.

Then the family would sing :
"Alegre, alegre
cacho fuo ven, tout ben ven
se sian pas maï, que signe pas men"
("Joy, joy
cacho fuo comes, everything good comes
and if we aren't more, then let us not be less")

Today, fireplaces are disappearing and the log has become a cake.

The women then invited everyone to the table.

And what a table !... A white tablecloth (or three, one on top of the other), lit with three candles and decorated with three plates of Saint Barbe wheat. The number three symbolizes the Holy Trinity. Wheat or lentils are the symbol of renewal and predict a good harvest. The prettiest plates are used, and there is always an extra one for the pauper who might come by the house.

According to each family's separate tradition, the dishes are either presented separately, or else brought all at once to the table.

One fish always presides : Cod. Depending on the region, eel, snails or sardines are added. Two vegetables also, are always present ; cardoons and spinach, cauliflower, marrow and celery also often appear :

Cardoons with Béchamel

Cooked with water, as with the preceding recipe, then placed in a dish with the Béchamel sauce, bake the cardoons in the oven with grated Gruyère.

The Béchamel can be made with butter or with olive oil (see recipe).

Cauliflower

It should be served in a gratin with a Béchamel sauce, or else raw with anchoïade.

Cardoons and anchovies

cardoons : 1 or 2

lemon : 1

anchovies : 7 or 8

flour,

olive oil, pepper, parsley

1 garlic clove

Peel and cut up the cardoons' ribs, place them in water with lemon as you go along.

Mix some water with two spoonfuls of flour in a cooking-pot. Bring to the boil and add the cardoon pieces.

Blanch them for 15 minutes (the flour will absorb their bitterness and make them whiter) and put them in a sieve under a strong tap, this will firm them up.

Also, fry the chopped onions in olive oil, with the garlic and the de-salted and de-boned anchovies.

Make a little roux with a spoonful of flour and add the cardoons. Stir and serve with grated and melted Gruyère.

Leek sauce

This is really Cod with leeks, a speciality of villages along the Calavon and in Haute Provence for the Gros Souper.

leeks : 6 lbs.

black olives : 7 oz.

cod : 2 bowlfuls, poached, de-salted 24 hours in advance, shredded

hard-boiled eggs : 2

olive oil, salt, pepper

dried bread crumbs : 1 bowlful

Poach for 5 minutes the leeks cut into 2-inch pieces (they will taste better if you poach them before cutting them up). Put them in a pan with 4 spoonfuls of olive oil, fry them until they form a cream, without colouring. Add the black olives, and poached cod. Cook, uncovered, on low heat for 40 minutes, without boiling. If it goes dry, add a little of the cod's cooking water. Cover the top with the dried bread crumbs : they will swell. When serving, stir everything up, season to taste. You might add cut-up hard-boiled eggs.

Marrow gratin

marrows : 1 lb.

onion : 1

flour : 2 spoonfuls

Gruyère, salt, pepper, olive oil

In a covered pan, fry the pieces of marrow in olive oil, add salt, pepper and a bay leaf. Put the marrow through a vegetable mill, once they have disgorged all their liquid. Mix with a sliced and browned onion, two beaten eggs, a little flour stirred into a little milk, a little nutmeg. Place the mixture in an oiled tian. Powder with grated cheese and cook for 30 minutes or more.

The desserts

There must be thirteen desserts, representing Jesus and the twelve apostles. According to the Marseilles tradition : raisins, dried figs, almonds and nuts, candied plums, pears, apples and citrus fruit, quince jam, white and black nougat, yellow melon, fougasse or "pompe". The dried fruit are called **"beggars"**, their colours resembling those of the beggar monks, carmelites, dominicans, benedictines and capuchins. A nut or almond pricked into a fig is called Capuchin nougat. Each family has its own personal tradition to add. Don't forget oranges, a sign of wealth, and clementines, often made into little oil lamps placed in front of the Crèche. A yellow melon, kept in the attic since September, is often used as one of the thirteen desserts, along with grapes that have drying upside-down since the beginning of the winter.

The first dessert is

the "Pompe"

a round flat cake made with fine flour and cooked with olive oil and orange-blossom, also known as **"Gibassier"**, depending on the region.

flour : 2 lbs.
sugar : 1/2 pound
baking yeast : 1 oz.
orange-blossom water : 1/2 glass
olive oil : 7 oz.
grated orange peel : 2

Mix and knead everything together. If it's too dry, add a little orange-blossom water. Place the ball of dough in a salad bowl, covered with a cloth, and leave it to rest for 3 hours, it will double in size. Then make a round flat pancake with it. Gouge it deeply. Bake it on low heat, watching over the cooking.

Never forget the :

Black and White Nougat

The recipe for white Nougat is very complicated. This is the recipe for Black Nougat, also known as "Black Nougat of Apt".

almonds : 2 lbs.

honey : 2 lbs.

papier hostie ("host paper") — you will find this in French "drogueries" around Christmas.

Sort the shelled almonds. Break a handful and leave the others intact.

Heat the honey very slowly in a copper or thick-bottomed pot, stirring with a wooden spoon. When it is about to boil the honey will change colour, it will take on a darker tone. Throw in the broken and whole almonds into the boiling honey. Turn and turn the mixture. When the almonds crack they "sing", stop the cooking. Pour the mixture into small, rectangular, not too thick moulds. Wait for it too be cold, then extract the Nougat from the moulds (a difficult job !)

Cut it into bars with a large sharp knife, or else... a power saw ! !... Careful of fingers !

The boiling mixture can also be poured onto "host paper". This is a delicate operation. Moisten the paper with a sponge to get it too fit into the mould. Pour the honey over it and cover with paper.

If I had you break the almonds, it was only to fill the mould more thoroughly ; the broken almonds will fit into the corners of the mould and be more evenly spread out through the Nougat. But this is not at all indispensable.

You could make yourself a wooden mould, with hooks on each of the four corners. You can then open it when the Nougat has cooled.

You could also make :

Praline nuts

> for : 1 glass of almonds,
> 1 glass of sugar
> 1/2 glass of water

Mix everything together in a casserole.

Put on a low heat, turn. Turn especially thoroughly once it comes to the boil, and the water evaporates. The almonds will crackle, the sugar will turn to caramel. Watch them carefully.

Then, remove them before they go too dark, toss them onto an oiled marble top and separate them very rapidly with a knife.

Many tarts enter into the Christmas desserts. Honey and almonds, compote tarts with pastry criss-crossing the top, sweet spinach tart (see recipe)

Today, the Oreillettes, that traditionally accompanied Carnival-time, are also to be found as part of the Gros Souper.

After the Supper, one always drinks a "vin cuit" with the desserts. These "cooked wines" are to be found in the specialized épiceries of Marseilles and other big towns.

Amongst the wines on the Palette label, Château Simone (Meyreuil) distinguishes itself by proposing, alongside its hearty Reds, elegant Whites and flavourful Rosés, a syrupy "vin cuit" that is appreciated as an accompaniment to the thirteen desserts. This wine is obtained by concentrating the must in cauldrons over heat.

Once supper is over, the table is not cleared. "Angels come to eat the crumbs"... And everyone leaves for midnight mass.

For your Notes

A picnic or lunch at the "cabanon"

There are different attitudes and different ways to fill your "biasse" (pouch).

You may content yourself with an old hunk of bread.

You may bring nothing at all and count on the generosity of your friends and neighbors.

You may bring nothing at all, knowing that your friend and neighbor will distribute plenty of good things as usual.

Or else, you may be the one distributing...

As well as olives (not too many, they make one thirsty), salami from Sault, crushed hard-boiled eggs, squashed tomatoes and melted butter, don't forget cold tomato, onion, omelettes, cold ratatouille, aubergine with tomato, slices of pork with sage... Local wines (beware of those that hit you in the legs, and prevent you from leaving...)... fruit and goat cheese !...

Avoid grilling meat, because of the risk of forest fires.

But how about bringing a :

Pan - bagnat

Take a large pain de campagne, or else small individual loaves (more practical).

Prepare a good salad of sliced tomatoes, sliced onion, anchovies, grilled sweet peppers, olives and garlic if you want, with basil or mint. Their must be plenty of vinaigrette.

Cut the loaf in two, lengthwise. One can also hollow out the Pain de campagne from one end. This is rather more work, but very satisfying when it comes to results. You fill the bread little by little, pressing down.

Soak the bread with the olive oil-dominated vinaigrette. Arrange the tomatoes, onions and anchovies on the one side of the bread and soak, then cover with the other half of the loaf, impregnated with olive oil. Squeeze the two halves together. Envelop the sandwich in a wet, wrung-out cloth. Remove the cloth just before leaving on your picnic, and wrap your Pan-bagnat in a tight piece of aluminium foil.

When serving, the loaf will be cut into as many slices as there are guests.

Variation : You can crush the salad, then place the mixture in the bread.

If you aren't taking plates, bring lots of paper towel, the Pan-bagnat will drip everywhere !....

A word of advice in choosing the wine

We went to see the Maître de Chais of the Delarozière-Dubrule Cellar, and here is the advice he gave us.

For the apéritif, alongside the home-made wines for which you have the recipes, you could propose a wine of the year, a fresh and fruity White or Rosé.

As a general rule, spicy and strongly seasoned dishes, or ingredients with strong tastes deserve a robust wine. The wine must "follow" and be in harmony with the dish.

One can choose a vintage wine or an old and "supple" Red.

Lighter-tasting dishes call for a wine of the year.

For salads, first courses, vegetables, choose according to your taste, a fresh and light White or Red of the year.

For delicate dishes, light and subtle tasting, choose a Red wine at most two-or three-years-old.

For vegetable mousses, subtle patés and foie-gras, use a one or two-year-old dry White wine. Red will be preferred with truffle omelettes.

Grilled meat requires rather a fruity Rosé or a light Red.

For fish, choose dry White, but a light Red wine, a two-or three-year-old "primeur"-type will go very well with grilled fish. For the Christmas "Gros souper", there is a particular "vin cuit" that I speak of in the relevant chapter.

And if you want more details, go and have a chat with the Cellar owners. They love their wines and will rapidly have you loving them too.

Home-made wines and liqueurs.

Often made with fruit and herbs, they make a housewife's reputation.

To be drunk as an apéritif :

Cherry - tree wine

for one litre of good red wine :
100 cherry-tree leaves
10 oz. of sugar
1 1/2 glasses of 45° eau-de-vie

Leave the ingredients to macerate for a week, filter and bottle.

Walnut wine

walnuts : 45, with their peel
red wine : 5 litres
sugar : 2 lbs.
eau-de-vie : 1/2 litre
vanilla : 1 pod
nutmeg, 4 cloves, cinnamon

Use gloves to handle the walnuts. Crush them, put them in the wine with the other ingredients, leave to macerate for 45 days, filter and bottle.

Orange wine

dry white wine : 5 litres
lemon : 1
oranges : 6
eau-de-vie : 1 litre
sugar : 2 lbs.

Cut the oranges and lemon into large pieces, with their skin. Put them into the wine with the eau-de-vie, and the sugar. Leave

to macerate for 45 days, shaking the recipient from time to time.
Filter and bottle.

Variation : *instead of oranges, use grapefruit.*

Peach wine

Rosé wine : 5 litres, 11 or 12° alcohol

peach-tree leaves : 600, picked between the 15th of August
and the 30th of September

eau-de-vie : 1 litre

sugar : 2 lbs.

vanilla : 1 pod

Leave the leaves to macerate in the wine with the eau-de-vie
and vanilla for 6 days. Remove the leaves, add the sugar, shake, filter
and bottle.

Sage wine

a good handful of flowers

a litre of eau-de-vie or Marc

40 days under the sun ; and moon, on the window-sill.

This wine, drunk in a liqueur glass, is a sovereign remedy against
fatigue and fainting spells… it shakes you up, in the same way as the…

Long-life eau-de-vie

eau-de-vie : 1 litre

Remove a quarter of the eau-de-vie from the bottle and fill the
space with rosemary, sage, thyme, marjoram, basil and mint. Leave
to macerate outside for 30 days. Don't remove the herbs and, every
year, add new ones.

A few drops a day, and you'll live to be a hundred...

Myrtle - berry wine

Cassis red wine : 5 litres
myrtle berries : 1 lb.
sugar : 2 lbs.
eau-de-vie : 1 litre
Crush the berries, macerate 60 days. Filter. Bottle.

Aspic wine

red wine : 3/4 in a full litre bottle
a handful of flowers
Infuse for 40 days. Filter.
Sovereign for intestinal troubles
along with...

Juniper eau - de - vie

eau-de-vie : 1/2 litre
juniper berries : a handful
Macerate the crushed berries for 40 days.

Vin cuit

traditional for the "Gros souper" (see chapter)

Rosemary eau-de-vie

eau-de-vie : 1 litre

a good handful of rosemary blossoms

Macerate 40 days, then add 7 oz. of sugar.

Very effective in draining the gall-bladder.

Guignolet

Stoned cherries : 2 lbs.

sugar : 7 oz.

vanilla : 1 pod

eau-de-vie : 1/2 litre

red wine : 2 litres

Cook the cherries with the sugar for 30 minutes. Put this through a sieve. For each half litre of juice pour in half a litre of eau-de-vie. Add the vanilla.

Leave it to macerate for 8 days.

Add the red wine.

Wait for two months before drinking.

Ratafia

the name itself is intoxicating....
and makes one wish to drink it and be merry !

Four-fruit Ratafia

blackberries, cherries, rasberries, red currants : 2 lbs. of
each

Crush half the cherry stones.
Crush the fruit, and mix them with the crushed almonds from
the stones. Leave to rest for three days in a cool place. Filter.
For a litre of juice :

a litre of eau-de-vie

a little cinnamon

4 oz. (or a little more) sugar

Macerate for 30 days. Bottle.

Cherry Ratafia

black cherries : 2 lbs.
eau-de-vie : 1 litre
sugar : 8 oz.

For every litre of juice : 8 oz of sugar, a little cinnamon.
Crush half the stones, crush their almonds with the cherries. Put
in a cool place for 24 hours. Macerate for 8 days. Bottle.

Muscat grape Ratafia

Crush some good-looking grapes. Put them through a sieve.
For every litre of juice :

a litre of eau-de-vie

10 oz. of sugar, a little cinnamon
Infuse 10 to 15 days. Filter. Bottle.
Warning ! Inspect the bottles from time to time to make sure there isn't any explosive fermentation ! Catastrophic for the environment...

Cherries in eau-de-vie

griotte cherries : 2 lbs.
sugar : 13 oz.
eau-de-vie : 1 litre

This preparation is made in two goes, with a five day interval.

Crush a pound of cherries with their stones, put them into the eau-de-vie for 5 days. Filter, throw away the residue. Put the sugar and intact Griottes into the coloured alcohol, after having pricked pin-holes in them, and cut their stems off half an inch from the fruit.

Wait for a few months before eating them.

Jam

The fig-tree is weighed down with figs, they are falling to the ground, and everything is sticky. The cherry Clafoutis can't absorb all the fruit from the orchard and the neighbor's melons are generously arriving everyday... Why not make jam ?
For you, for your friends, for some never-ending breakfasts...

Apricot and vanilla jam

> apricots : 4 lbs.
> sugar : 4 lbs.
> water : 1 pt.
> vanilla : 1 pod

Pour the sugar, water and halved vanilla into a pot. Bring to the boil for three minutes.

Toss the cut up fruit into the pot. Bring to a strong boil, stir, cook for three-quarters of an hour. To check the cooking, take a drop that should congeal at once.

Cherry jam

> cherries : 2 lbs.
> sugar : 26 oz.
> water : 7 fl. oz. for every two pounds of sugar

Stone the cherries. Cook water and sugar together and add the cherries. Cook for 25 minutes. Check the cooking with a droplet that must congeal.

Lemon jelly

> 4 untreated lemons
> 2 pints of water
> 2 pounds of sugar

Cut the lemons into very very small fine pieces. Leave them to soak for 24 hours in the water.

The next day, cook the water and lemons for 3/4 of an hour and add the sugar. Leave this to rest for 24 hours.

The last day, cook for 1/4 of an hour and put the jelly into pots.

Quince jelly

quinces : 4 lbs.
sugar : 13 oz. per pint of juice
lemons : 1 per two pints of juice
muslin

Wipe the quinces well. Peel them. Remove the hard heart and pips and save them in the tied up muslin, with the peelings. Put the quinces cut into eight into a large pot with water (about a pound of fruit for 2 pints of water). Bring to a fast boil, then lower the heat. The quinces must cook without squashing. Pour into a sieve, wring out the muslin, the jelling agent in the pips will come out thick and gluey. Put the quinces aside to make paste. For the jelly, put the collected juice through a linen and measure it. Put it back in the pot and heat. Add 13 ounces of sugar for every pint of juice, and the juice of one lemon for every two pints of juice. Cook on high heat, stirring often, and removing the scum. The jelly will be cooked after thirty minutes. The jelly should form a sheet , not droplets. Put it in pots. Cover immediately.

Quince paste

quinces cooked in the jelly
same weight of sugar

Cook the moistened sugar until it breaks like glass. Add the crushed quinces. Cook and reduce on strong heat until a spoonful of paste doesn't lose its shape, when falling back into the pot. Pour onto an oiled marble slab, or else into an oiled rectangular mould. Press it down into about an inch thickness. Let it rest in a dry place for 10 days. Remove it from the mould, cut the paste into sticks or squares. Roll them in cristallized sugar. Keep them in a metal tin. They will be delicious at Christmas.

Fig jam

figs : 6 lbs.

lemons : 4

sugar : 3 bottles of cane sugar syrup

Plunge the figs, peeled and stalks removed if you have the time, into a pot of boiling water for three minutes. Remove them and place them in a sieve. Pass them quickly under cold water, halve them. Pour the sugarcane syrup into the pot and bring to the boil. Then add the figs, lemon peel and juice. Cook on low heat for an hour and fifteen minutes. Watch the cooking.

Melon jam

melons : 2 lbs., peeled

sugar : 6 oz. for every two pounds of fruit

1/2 a glass of lemon juice, vanilla

Let the diced melon drain in a sieve. Put the fruit, sugar, vanilla and lemon juice into a pot. Boil for an hour. Put into pots.

Rasberries may be added : 1 lb. for every 4 lbs.

Blackberry jam

blackberries : 2 lbs.

sugar : 1&1/2 lbs.

water : 2 glasses

lemon : the juice from 1

Cook the water and sugar. Add the blackberries and lemon juice. Stir.

Check the cooking : a few drops must congeal at once on a cold plate. Put into pots. Leave to cool. Cover when cold.

Black jam

figs, pears, aubergines, melons, walnuts and quinces.

Boil a large quantity of figs. Put them in a cloth or sieve and drain. Toss the diced pears, melons and walnut quarters into the juice and boil. When cooked, the juice will become thick and black.

You can add whatever fruit you like, according to your fancy. Also according to your taste, the pieces can be large, small or not exist at all if you put the fruit through a mill.

Onion and Grenadine chutney

onions : 3 or 4 (about a pound)
strong vinegar (vinaigre vieux) : 3 tbsps.
old wine : 1 glass
Grenadine syrup : 1 tbsp.
sugar, butter, salt, pepper

Fry the onion rings in butter. Add sugar, salt, a pinch of taste if you want and Grenadine. Check the seasoning.

Cook, covered, for 20 minutes, slowly.

Add the vinegar, the wine and cook for 10 minutes. Excellent with hot or cold meat. The relish can be served hot or cold.

"Petit grelot" onion chutney

Grelot onions : 20 oz.
cane sugar : 10 oz.
lime : 1
dry white wine : 3&1/2 fl. oz.
vinegar : 3 1/2 fl. oz.
salt, pepper

Peel the onions, put them in a heavy-bottomed pan with the sugar and lime juice. Start the cooking slowly, so as to obtain a light caramel. Moisten with the white wine and vinegar. Add a little grated lime peel, salt and (a pinch of) pepper. Cook slowly until the liquid has entirely evaporated. Excellent with grilled or cold meat.

Watermelon or "Gigérine" jam

(or Gingérine)

This is not the North African watermelon with its red flesh and black pips, but a long lighter or darker marbled green watermelon, that is especially grown around Apt for jam.

Cut the watermelon into very very fine pieces. Remove the skin and seeds. Weigh the pieces and add half their weight in sugar.

Macerate for at least 12 hours.

The next day, cook them on low heat with the juice and peel from three lemons for 1/2 an hour from when the mixture starts to boil.

Cook like this for three days running. The jam will cristallize and become translucent.

I add ground ginger (1&1/2 tsps.) or freshly grated (1 tsp.)

Pear and spice chutney

pears : 6 lbs.

sugar : 3 lbs. granulated sugar

lemon : 1

cloves : 5

vanilla : 1 pod

fresh ginger : 1

Cut the peeled pears into not too thick slices. Let them macerate for 12 or 24 hours with the lemon juice and sugar. Drain them. Cook the juice for ten minutes.

Add the fruit with the cloves, the split vanilla, the grated ginger and cook for 30 minutes, from boiling, on low heat.

Put into pots. Cover when cold.

Excellent with cold meat, rice, etc...

Pumpkin jam

so pretty !...

> pumpkin : 6 lbs. peeled and diced
> sugar : 6 lbs.
> 3 oranges
> 3 lemons

Cook the sugar with a little water until the juice breaks like glass.

Add the pumpkin, the lemon peel and the orange and lemon juice. Cook, stirring, until the pumpkin is almost melting. Pour into a sieve. Then reduce the juice a little and add the pumpkin. Boil for 5 minutes. Wait for it to be cooler before putting the jam in pots, and cover the next day.

Green tomato chutney

> green tomatoes : 4 lbs.
> sugar : 2 1/4 lbs.
> lemons : 4
> fresh ginger : a little piece of root, or ground : 2 tsps.

In a terrine, arrange a layer of very very finely cut tomatoes, a layer of sugar. Leave to macerate twenty-four hours.

Put this into a pot with the water from the maceration, the juice of the four lemons, the grated or ground ginger.

Bring slowly to the boil and cook for one and three-quarter hours from boiling point. The juice must set like a jelly. Put into pots.

Bachelor's jam

This is not a jam, but a flamboyant cocktail of fruit in alcohol. The preparation requires two months.

Choose a large and very pretty glass jar. Fill it with a good white alcohol : Marc de Provence or... Vodka.

Choose summer fruit, ripened on the branch.

As they appear, arrange them delicately in the jar in the proportions of a pound of sugar per pound of fruit.

Start with strawberries, then cherries — stoned or not — rasberries, quartered apricots, yellow and white peaches, cut into thick slices, greengage or Reine-Claude plums, nice and firm diced pears, golden Chasselas grapes and black muscat grapes.

Use your imagination to add many other varieties...

Don't stir the fruit in the jar.

Watch out that the children don't eat too many !

Wait for two or three months before tasting...

Recommendations : Wipe the fruit thoroughly, if you wash them. If the mixture ferments a little, don't worry, it's perfectly normal. Serve them after coffee, in nice glasses or small cups.

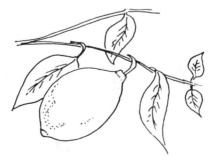

For your Notes

Index

Printed and bound in Barcelona, Spain by Cronion, S.A.